Science
Progress Papers
2

Answer Book

A J and M D Thomas

Nelson

Thomas Nelson and Sons Ltd
Nelson House   Mayfield Road
Walton-on-Thames   Surrey
KT12 5PL   UK

51 York Place
Edinburgh
EH1 3JD   UK

Thomas Nelson (Hong Kong) Ltd
Toppan Building 10/F
22A Westlands Road
Quarry Bay   Hong Kong

Thomas Nelson Australia
102 Dodds Street
South Melbourne
Victoria 3205
Australia

Nelson Canada
1120 Birchmount Road
Scarborough   Ontario
M1K 5G4   Canada

© A. J. and M. D. Thomas 1990

First published by Thomas Nelson and Sons Ltd 1990

ISBN 0-17-423181-4
NPN 987654321 } Pupils' Book

ISBN 0-17-423182-2
NPN 98765432 } Answer Book

Printed in Great Britain by Ebenezer Baylis and Son Ltd

CONTENTS

NOTES TO TEACHERS, PARENTS AND PUPILS

Notes to teachers and parents

1 Science surrounds today's children and is as much part of their life as numerical skill or the spoken or written word. Just as thoughts cannot be expressed or discussed until the basic skills of language are mastered, science cannot be understood without a basic grasp of the ideas and vocabulary of science.

2 These papers are designed to develop the scientific literacy of children between the ages of 10 and 14 by exposing them to the vocabulary and ways of thinking of the scientific community in an interesting and relaxed way. The papers cover a large proportion of the **National Curriculum**, which places Science alongside English Language and Mathematics as a core subject, and they also provide valuable preparation for the **Common Entrance** examination.
The papers have not been divided into the subject areas physics, chemistry and biology, as some contain a mixture of two or three subjects, and some are dedicated to just one. It should be clear from the title of each paper which topics are covered.

3 There are two books of Science Progress Papers, which are designed as a pair, with many of the ideas in *Science Progress Papers 1* being developed further in *Science Progress Papers 2*. It will be advisable for all but the most scientifically experienced students to work through *Science Progress Papers 1* before approaching *Science Progress Papers 2*.

4 The papers are not intended just for schoolwork but aim to give pleasure to both parents and children in exploring the fascinating world of science together.

5 The questions are not meant primarily for assessment purposes, but as a means of illuminating the text and asking for an observational response. Some of them are open-ended questions which are not easily marked, while others have a range of possible answers. Nevertheless, the number of points scored on a paper will indicate how well the topic has been understood and measure the student's progress.
Please note that some of the experiments described are not suitable for children.

Instructions to pupils

(a) Read each paper carefully, taking as long as you need to understand what has been discussed.

(b) Read each question carefully and look for the answer first in the discussion which comes before it in the paper.

(c) Where possible try to find out the answer by performing an experiment. Some experiments are suggested – you might think of others for yourself.

(d) Look for the answer in books – others may have discovered it before you have.

(e) Never be afraid to ask other people for help.

(f) If you find it difficult to express the answer to some questions in words, draw a diagram to convey your meaning. There is often space in the text.

It is best to perform experiments only when a teacher or parent is present.

REMEMBER! If you don't know the answer to a question, do as scientists have always done – observe, experiment, record, and read what others discovered before you.

A.J.T.

Some of the materials around us are natural; others are synthetic or artificial. Plastics are synthetic. They are made from relatively cheap and plentiful raw materials, often from oil.

Plastics can be easily used to make cheap and sturdy waterproof articles, and plastic containers, boxes and buckets are in use all over the world.

Plastics are rapidly replacing glass, metal, pottery and other materials, often providing cheaper substitutes, sometimes better than the originals.

[1–9]

Look at this picture. How many products made of natural materials are shown? List them: _Milk jug, cricket bat, shopping basket, cook book_

How many things can you see that are most probably plastic? List them:

Nylon tights, rubbish bin, hair dryer, telephone, toothbrush

States of things

[10–21]
Materials can be solids, liquids or gases. These are called the **states** of the material. The state of a material can vary according to its temperature.

Water is one of the most familiar materials.

10–12 If water gets very cold it can ..freeze.. and change its state into ..a solid.. that we call ..ice..

13–15 This state can be changed back to a ..liquid.. when it ..melts.. and the solid becomes ..water..

16–18 If we heat the water even more it ..boils.. and forms ..steam.. which is a ..gas (or ..vapour)..

When a material is hot enough to be in the gaseous state it is often called a **vapour**. Thus, we often call steam 'water vapour'.

You can encounter water in all three states – solid, liquid and gas – in your own kitchen. With more extreme changes of temperature most materials can be seen to change state.

19–21 Iron heated in a furnace ..melts.. and becomes a ..liquid.. . When it cools down again it becomes a ..solid.. once more.

[22–27]
Underline the correct word from the ones in brackets each time.

When we change the state of water from liquid to solid we make it (hotter, colder). This involves the (addition, removal, dissolving) of (heat, salt, substances). To change the liquid to a gaseous state, which we call a (wind, vapour, cloud, helium), we must (heat, freeze, stir, shake) the liquid until it (cools, boils, moves, turns grey).

[28–31]
Pure liquids always freeze at the same temperature. If you dissolve other substances in the liquid, it will lower the temperature at which it freezes and raise the temperature at which it boils. This can be very useful.

28 Why are icy roads salted in winter? ..The salt lowers the freezing point so that.. ..ice melts..

29 Why add antifreeze to car radiators in winter? .To prevent the water from.. .freezing when the car is cold..

30 Why does a river estuary rarely freeze, even when it cold enough for fresh water lakes to freeze? .The salt of the sea lowers its freezing point..

31 These plastic pots of water have both been in a freezer for the same time.

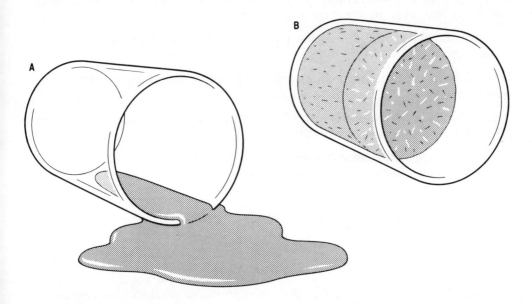

Which one has salt dissolved in the water? .A..

[32–37]
Are the following statements true or false?

32 Rocks cannot melt. .False..

33 Metals can melt. .True..

34 Gases cannot be liquified. .False..

35 All liquids freeze at the same temperature. .False..

36 One kilo of a substance occupies the same volume whether it is a solid, liquid or gas. .False..

37 When a liquid evaporates in a closed space the expansion which takes places can exert a physical 'push'. .True..

How things conduct heat

[38–46]

Some materials conduct heat more readily than others.

Place a metal spoon in a cup of hot tea. The handle of the spoon soon becomes too hot to touch.

The handle of a plastic spoon in hot tea remains cool for much longer.

Metals are generally good **conductors** of heat, with aluminium and copper being among the best. Heat moves easily through them.

Most plastics, wood and glass conduct heat relatively poorly and are called **insulators**.

Heat takes time to travel through a conductor; and the more material there is to travel through the longer the heat will take.

A metal spoon in hot water will quickly become too hot to hold near to the water. It takes considerably longer before the tip of the handle becomes very hot.

The thickness of an **insulator** or **conductor** is therefore important. It is best to use *several* layers of a tea-towel when carrying a hot plate!

Are the following statements true or false?

38 All substances transfer heat equally. ....False...

39 Metals transfer heat more easily than wood. ..True...

40 Some metals transfer heat more readily than others. ...True..

Glass and brick are roughly equally good insulators, but glass windows are much thinner than bricks.

41 Less heat is lost from a room through $2\,m^2$ of window than through an equal area of brick wall. ...False..

Air is one of the best insulators known, but it moves. We can only make use of air as an insulator if we can trap it.

42 Birds fluff out their feathers in cold weather and cats look bigger when it is frosty. How does this help them to keep warm? .A layer of air is trapped in the fur. .or feathers.

43 How does a woollen blanket or a feather duvet keep us warm? ..By trapping a layer.. ..of air next to us.

44–45 How does double glazing of windows reduce the heat lost through them? ...It traps a layer of air. and ..there are two layers of glass..

46 Why are two blankets warmer than one? ..They provide twice the thickness of.. ..insulating material.

[47–48]

A is a copper bar, B a wooden bar, C a glass bar and D a steel bar.

They are all the same size and shape and equally immersed in the boiling water.
The marbles are attached to the bars by a blob of wax.

The wax will melt as soon as it gets warm, and the marbles will fall off.

47 Which marble do you think will drop off first? ...A.

48 Which do you think will stay attached longest? ...B.

The elasticity of things

[49–54]

If we take a rubber ball and squeeze it, it returns to its original shape when we let go.

If we squeeze a ball of plasticine it stays in the shape we have pressed it into.

If we drop the rubber ball it bounces. If we drop the plasticine ball it lands 'splat' and remains on the floor.

The rubber ball has a high degree of **elasticity**. The plasticine ball has not.

Similarly, if we stretch a rubber band and release it it assumes its original length. A length of cotton will break rather than stretch. The rubber band has a higher degree of elasticity.

We can use what we know and experience about the properties of materials when we need to design and make things.

Let's suppose that we want to experiment with toy parachutes and have a competition to see how far they will travel in the wind. We will need to make a parachute that will descend fairly slowly.

We will also need to make something which will send it as high as possible into the air. A catapult might be the best way of sending a folded parachute into the air.

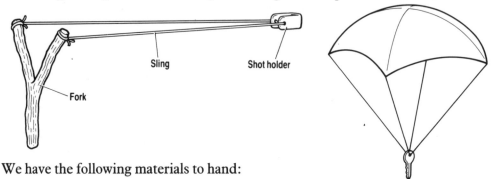

We have the following materials to hand:

rubber cord   polythene bags   wood   string   cotton thread   metal key
square of silk   piece of soft leather   steel-wire coathanger

The parachute needs a light bell or canopy with a small weight attached. It must be possible to roll it into a small ball to be launched into the air by the catapult.

49   What might be best to use for the canopy of the parachute? ..Square.of.silk...

50   What would you choose to represent the weight of the person on the parachute?
      ..Metal.key....

51   What would you choose to attach the weight to the canopy? .Cotton thread..

52   What material might be the best to use for the fork of the catapult? ...Wood..

53   What would you choose to make the sling? ..Rubber.cord..

54   The shot holder could be made from .piece.of.soft.leather....

The density of materials

[55–62]
Suppose we weigh a large glass marble and choose an apple of the same weight.

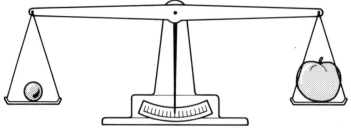

Underline your answers to questions 55–56 from the words in brackets.

55   If we put the marble into a beaker full of water it will (float, <u>sink</u>).

56 If we put the apple into water it will (<u>float</u>, sink).

Both objects weigh the same amount but are they the same size?

57 Which is the larger? .The apple....

It has the greater **volume**. It weighs the same but is less dense than the other object.

The *weight* of objects may change. Things can become weightless in space. But their *mass* stays the same. An astronaut has the same mass whether on the ground or in space!

The apple and the large glass marble have the same mass but different volumes, so their **density** will be different.

We can describe the density of an object by dividing its mass by its volume.

If we take a number of apples of different sizes we can measure the volume of each of them by taking a litre measuring jug and filling it with water to the 500 ml mark.

Then put the apple in the water and hold it under with a pencil.

Reading the new volume of the water will give the volume of the apple plus the water which was already there, so we can calculate the volume of the apple.

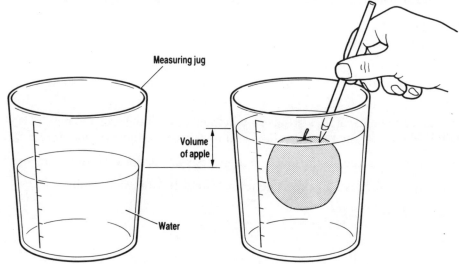

We can measure its mass by weighing it. Then we can calculate its density. If we made the same measurements for a number of different sizes of apple:

58 Would you expect the densities of all the apples to be different? .No...

59 How could you measure the density of water? ..Weigh a measured volume of water..

60 Would you expect it to be more or less than the density of an apple? .More...

61 How could you measure the density of a glass marble? ..Weigh it and measure the.....
....volume by the amount of water it displaces..

62 Would you expect the glass marble to be more or less dense than water? ..More...

Strength of materials

[63–66]

Some materials are strong and stiff and do not easily break or bend. Others are strong and pliable, and bend but do not easily break. Some materials have very little physical strength, breaking easily.

Again, some materials are strong and light, others are strong and heavy while some are weak and heavy.

Underline your answers from the words in brackets.

63 A plastic ruler is fairly strong and (stiff, <u>pliable</u>).

64 A pencil is strong and (<u>stiff</u> , pliable).

65 A paper tissue (is strong, is stiff, <u>has very little physical strength</u>).

66 An iron bar is strong, stiff and (pliable, light, <u>heavy</u>).

If we can classify the strength of materials we can put them to the best use. Tests of pulling strength, bending strength and resistance to tearing will tell us which material would be best for a climbing frame, a rope ladder or a diving board.

We will also notice that the shape of the material affects its strength too.

[67–71]

We can test for:

resistance to pulling, or **tensile strength** – whether something stretches or breaks. If it stretches, does it return to its original shape when the force is removed? Does it recover?

resistance to bending, or **stiffness** – whether something breaks or bends. If it bends, does it straighten when the bending force is removed? Does it recover?

resistance to tearing. Is the material more resistant in one direction than another?

67 This picture suggests an experiment for testing resistance to ..pulling..

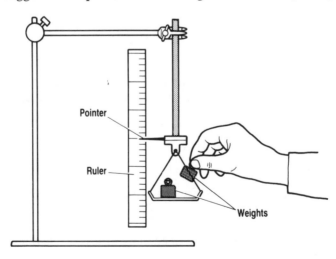

68 Can you measure recovery with the same arrangement? ...Yes..

69 Can you suggest an experiment to measure bending? Draw a picture.

......Add weights and measure the bending distance...

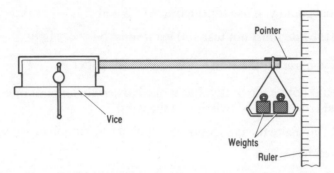

70 Add to the drawing what you would need to measure the recovery from bending.

...Remove the weights and see whether the pointer goes back to its original position...

71 You find that a woven material tears more easily in one direction than the other. Can you explain this?

....There are more or stronger fibres in one direction than in the other......................

The right material for the job

[72–81]
We can learn a considerable amount about materials. Some have more suitable properties for a particular job than others.

You might plan to make a kite.

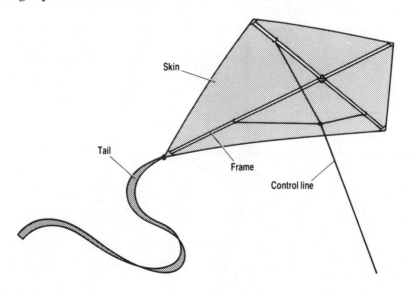

72 A kite needs to be ..light.and.stiff.. to fly well.

73 It also needs to be .strong... because it gets buffeted by the wind.

74 To resist bending in the wind the frame has to be ..stiff..

75 What material could you use for the frame? ..Wood...

76 The skin of the kite must not tear and yet it must be ..very.light...

77 What could you use for the skin? .Silk,.nylon.or..paper....

The tail should not be too bulky, but it needs a certain amount of weight to balance the kite. It also does a lot of twisting in the wind.

78 What could you make the tail from? .Strip.of.cloth,.ribbon.or.string.with.a.certain. amount of weight tied on

Finally, the line which controls the kite should be light so that the kite is not weighed down by it.

79–80 It should not .break.... or .stretch... or you will lose the kite.

81 A suitable choice for the line would be .string...

[82–88]
Suppose you are asked to design a swing for the school playground. Look at the various parts of a swing.

The cross-beam should not bend or break.

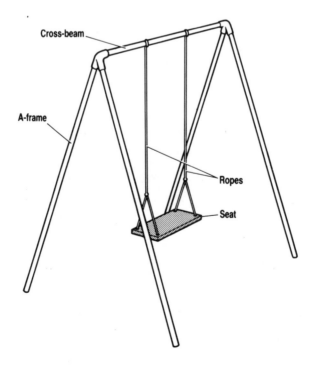

82 It could be made from ..wood.or.metal.tube..

83 The A-frame supports should be strong against ..bending..

84 How could the A-frames be prevented from digging into the ground? By putting
..them to press on a large, flat surface, like a wooden board

85 What property would you look for in choosing the material to make the seat?
..It.needs.to.be.strong.and.stiff,.not.to.bend

86 It could be made of ..wood..

87 The ropes should not break nor should they ..stretch..

88 Add to the drawing an extra support to make the swing stronger and less likely to
collapse.

[89–91]
You are also asked to design a see-saw for the school playground. You are given a
plank of wood, an old oil drum and some bricks.

89 Draw a picture showing how you could use these objects.

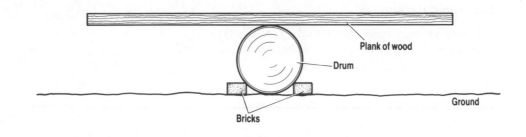

90 What particular property would the plank need?
..It.should.not.bend.or.break

91 What particular property would the oil drum need?
..It.should.not.be.crushed.by.the.force.bearing.down.on.it

Everything we 'do' in the physical world involves some form of energy being 'used'.

When we talk about 'using' energy what is happening is that energy is being changed from one form into another. As a result work is being done.

Car engines convert the chemical energy of petrol into the mechanical energy of movement and the electrical energy of the lights and radio. Cars also produce heat energy and a lot of sound energy.

Plants 'use' energy from the sun (**solar** energy) in the form of **light**. They combine it with water and minerals from the soil and carbon dioxide from the air, and produce **starches** and **sugars**.

These are like basic 'fuels' or foods for animals. When animals eat plants, or other animals, 'burning' the starch in their food releases its stored energy for work by muscles (**mechanical** energy), or as **chemical** energy to be used in body growth and repair.

In animals, excess energy is often stored as fat.

[1–6]
Here is a list of animal functions. Put a tick by the ones which you think use energy, and a cross by the ones which don't.

Circulation of the blood ....✓............   Using muscles ....✓................

Thinking ....✗................   Breathing ....✓................

Digesting food ....✓................   Sweating ....✗................

[7–12]
I have two cats called Stockwell and Jemima. They are both about the same age.

Stockwell is very large, ginger tabby, and lazy.
Jemima is sleek, small, ginger, always rushing around inside and out and often hunting.

Although they both eat a tin of the same cat food every day, Stockwell weighs almost twice as much as Jemima.

Can you suggest any possible reasons why this should be? ...Stockwell may be male

...and male cats tend to be bigger. Jemima expends a lot of energy rushing around.

...Stockwell is lazy and doesn't waste much energy. Jemima uses more energy

...keeping warm as she is out more often. Jemima may be a smaller type of cat

...naturally.

Forces – inertia

A great deal of energy is used around the world just to make things move.

A ball lying on level ground will not move unless it is kicked.

If you are standing on a bus you will notice that as the bus moves off you tend to fall backwards, and as the bus slows down again you will be thrown forward.

All things want to stay as they are. This is known as **inertia**.

To start a stationary object moving, or to stop a moving object, requires the use of a **force**. A force is also needed to change the direction of a moving object.

[13–18]
Which would you think is the easiest trolley:

13 to start moving? ..The empty trolley...

14 to steer? ..The empty trolley...

15 to stop? ..The empty trolley...

16 How important do you think weight is in these? ...Very important...

17 How important do you think speed is? ...Not as important as weight...

18 Does a light object have more inertia than a heavy one? ..No....

Force of gravity

[19–23]
If we throw a dart or catapult a stone, they do not keep going for ever, but slow down and fall to the ground.
Another force must be acting to slow them down and a third force to make them fall to the ground.

19 What force do you think causes them to slow down? ...Air.resistance. (A clue to this one – try waving a piece of paper!)

20 Why does a spacecraft in space not slow down in the same way? ...There.is.no.air.in. ...space..

21 What force do you think causes the dart or stone to fall to the ground? .The.force.. .of.gravity..

22 Can you think why a ball will drop to the floor if you let it go? .The.force.of... ..gravity..

23 Why will a penny drop to the floor faster than a piece of paper? ...Air.resistance.. ..slows.down.the.paper..

[24–28]

24 Have you ever tried to run and slide on the ice? What happens?...You.can.slide.well

25 If you try to do the same thing on a summer day in the school playground, what will happen?..You.can.hardly.slide.at.all.

26 How good is a polished floor for sliding on? ...Usually.fairly.good.

In each of these cases a force acts to slow you down. Sometimes the force is very strong, sometimes weak. This force is known as **friction**. Friction is a force that acts to slow or stop movement.

27 If you rub your skirt or trousers vigorously with your hand, what happens to your hand? ..It.gets.warm..

28 So that we can see that the force of friction absorbs energy, changing it to ..heat.

We can easily see that when we slide on a slippery surface, more of the energy we use to push off will be used as motion than on a rough surface – we will slide more **efficiently.**

Similarly, machines will convert other forms of energy to mechanical use more efficiently if the various parts rub as little as possible. So the parts should be smooth and lubricated.

You can prove this by oiling a rusty bicycle and seeing how much easier it is to pedal.

Oil is a good lubricant on some surfaces; water may be a lubricant on others. But you won't want to cut down friction by watering your bike!

[29–30]
So we can see that we have to use energy to apply a force to start things moving, and that moving things have more energy than stationary ones.

Another force is then needed to change the direction of the moving object. If we throw a stone, the force of gravity changes its direction and pulls it back towards the earth.

The resistance of the air, or friction, produces a force which slows down moving objects. As this happens, some of their energy is absorbed as heat.

29 Why do the brakeblocks of a bicycle get hot when the brakes are applied going downhill? The force of friction turns mechanical energy into heat

30 Why does a spacecraft heat up and need to be protected from heat and burning as it re-enters the earth's atmosphere? There is friction with the air in the earth's atmosphere

A   B

[31–33]

31 Assuming these two lorries carry the same load at the same speed, which would you expect to use more fuel? B

32 Which would be more efficient? A

33 The less efficient lorry would waste more energy to push the air in its path

Levers

The amount of force required to lift a 25 kg weight from the floor to a table is probably as much as we can manage without help, but there are many ways in which we can lift much heavier things.

[34–43]

Suppose we take a 30 cm ruler and place a pencil under it on a flat surface such as a table. We will find that it balances when the pencil is at the centre of the ruler, at the 15 cm mark.

If we then place a 1p coin at one end, the 0 cm mark, and another on the 30 cm mark, the ruler will still balance.

34 If we move one coin to the 7.5 cm mark, where will the other coin need to be placed for the ruler to balance? At the 22.5 cm mark

–36 If we now place two 1p coins at the 7.5 cm mark, can we make the ruler balance with just one other 1p coin? Yes If so, where will the other coin need to be placed? At the 30 cm mark

These coins are trying to turn or **rotate** the ruler around the pencil. The point the pencil is at is called a **pivot** or **fulcrum.**

The coins are exerting a force on the ruler. We can see that one coin can balance two coins when it is placed twice as far from the pivot as the two coins. So the turning force on the ruler must depend both on the weight of the coins and on the distance they are from the pivot.

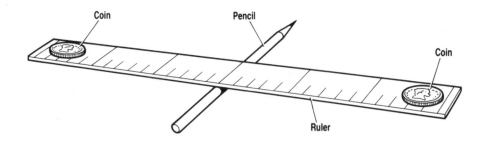

This turning force is called the **moment** of the force. The two moments acting on opposite sides of the pivot are opposing each other and so they cancel out – the ruler balances.

Underline your answer to question 37 from the answers in brackets.

37 From the experiment that we have just done we can say that the moment of a force is equal to the force (multiplied by, divided by, added to) its distance from the pivot.

38 Suppose we put three 1p coins at the 10 cm mark, with the pencil still under the 15 cm mark. Where can we place a single 1p coin to make the ruler balance?

   ..At the 30 cm mark..

By applying this method it is possible to move and lift objects which are far too heavy to lift directly.

This is called a **lever.** There are several possible arrangements, but always the force × the distance to the pivot = the moment.

Here the pivot is at some point between the two forces. One – in this case the rock – is called the **load.** The other – the lifting force being applied – is called the **effort.**

Again, these are examples of the lever, but here the fulcrum is at one end, the applied force (the effort) is at the other end, and the load is in the middle.

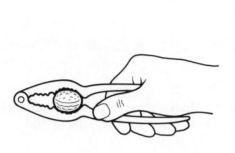

In this case the fulcrum is still at one end, but the load is at the other end and the effort applied at some point between.

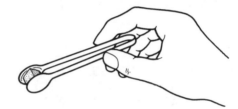

–43 Underline the items in this list which use a lever:

kitchen scales   knife sharpener   vacuum cleaner   hammer   whisk
<u>scissors</u>   pan and brush   <u>bottle opener</u>   floor polisher   <u>knife</u>
<u>bicycle brake</u>

Wheel and axle

[44–47]
We can use the idea of the lever in a rather different way.

Here the bucket containing the water is the load, the axle of the drum is the pivot and the effort is being applied through the handle.

Underline your answers from the answers in brackets.

4–45 What effect does the radius of the drum have? If the radius is small the handle will be (<u>easier</u>, more difficult) to turn. If it is large, turning the handle will be (easier, <u>more difficult</u>).

46 A long handle makes it (<u>easier</u>, more difficult) to
wind up the bucket.

47 It takes (<u>more</u>, less) turns of the handle to wind up
the bucket if the drum is small.

Chains, sprockets and gears

[48–52]
Pulling down to lift heavy weights is a lot easier than pulling up. A rope over a tree
branch, pulled down, will lift a weight much more easily than picking up the
weight directly.

The small wheel has a diameter of 10 cm, the large wheel has a diameter of 100 cm
and the engine weighs 200 kg. So the moment produced by the weight of the engine
will be 200 kg × 10 cm = 2000 kg/cm.

48 To balance this moment the mechanic will have to produce an equal moment on the
large wheel. The force (or pull) he will have to make on the chain to the large wheel
will be ...20... kg × 100 cm, which will be quite easy for him.

49 The circumference of the large wheel will be 100 cm × π and the circumference of
the small wheel will be 10 cm × π. So to lift the engine by 1 m he will have to pull
...10.. m length of his chain.

In making the job easier the mechanic has to work for longer. This is the general rule for machines – in reducing the force necessary to make the job possible, the work has to be done for longer.

50 What other force might increase the effort that the mechanic has to make?

...Friction, if he doesn't oil the wheel and axle...

Similar arrangements can use ropes and drums, chains and toothed wheels which are called **sprockets**, or toothed wheels which work on each other and are called **gears**. Toothed wheels where the teeth work on each other are said to be **meshed**. Rubber belts are frequently used with wheels with a grooved rim, called **pulleys**.

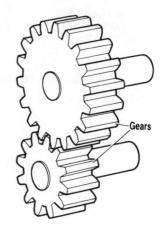
Gears

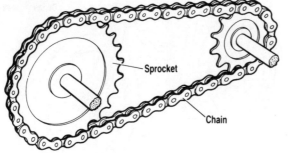
Sprocket
Chain

51 Can you think of an example of a chain and sprocket on a familiar object?

...On a bicycle...

52 Can you think of another common example of gears? ..Clock/car gearbox...

Ramps and inclined planes

[53–61]
Suppose you are pulling a heavy garden roller along the road and you come to a high step to the pavement. You are suddenly stopped and unable to lift the weight of the roller the 10 cm onto the pavement.

You can place a long plank against the step and the road and pull the roller up the ramp that is formed. This kind of ramp is often called an **inclined plane**.

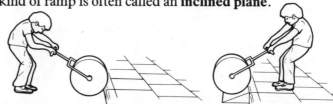

53 Will a long plank make the task easier than a short one? ..Yes...

54 How does it work? ...It spreads the lifting over a longer distance...

Underline your answer from the words in brackets.

55 The ramp makes the job take (shorter, <u>longer</u>) than a sudden lift.

56–61 Underline the items in the list below which use the same idea:

<u>gate latch</u>   <u>window wedge</u>   screwdriver   <u>chisel</u>   wrench
bicycle brake   <u>pencil sharpener</u>   <u>self-latching</u> door catch   <u>screw</u>

[62–71]
Look at this picture of a bicycle:

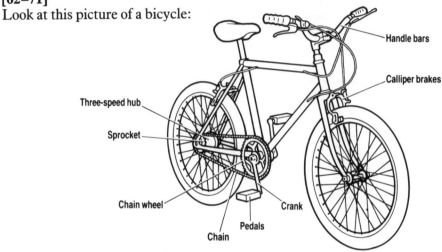

62 Draw a square around an example of a lever.

63 Draw a circle around an example of gears.

64 Draw a triangle around an example of chain and sprockets.

65 Would a long crank make the bicycle easier to pedal uphill? ...Yes...

Which of these arrangements would you prefer on your bicycle for each of the following? Write the picture's letter in the space:

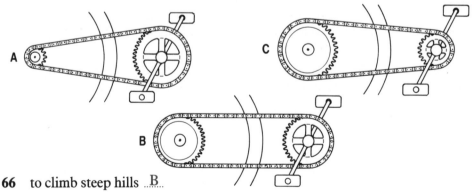

66 to climb steep hills ..B..

67 to ride along a straight level road with the wind behind you ..A..

68 to ride very slowly and perform tricks ..C..

69 Which arrangement would enable you to achieve the highest speed, if you were strong enough? ...A...

70 What is the advantage of having many different gears on your bicycle?
...To provide the right amount of effort for different conditions.

71 Why is it an advantage to have dropped handlebars and to bend low over them when going fast? ...It reduces the wind resistance...

Lenses

[1–8]
Glass and other transparent substances bend or **refract** light. We can use this effect in many different ways.

A piece of transparent material with at least one rounded surface forms a **lens**.

A lens with a surface curved in towards the edges is called a **convex** lens. The bending effect of the material causes the light beams to **converge**, or come together.

A lens with a surface which curves in towards the centre is called a **concave** lens. The bending effect causes the light beams to **diverge**, or spread.

A simple convex lens makes parallel light rays converge into a single point, which is called the **focus**.

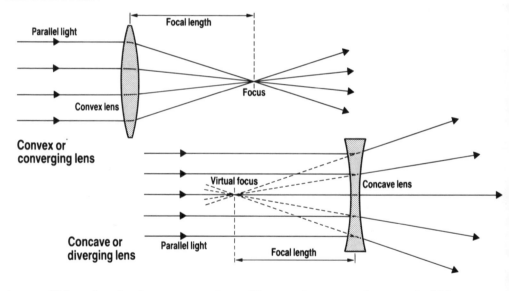

A magnifying glass is a large convex lens. If, on a nice sunny day, you hold it at right angles to the sun and hold a piece of paper beneath it, you can move the paper towards or away from the lens until the rays of the sun are **focused** as a small point.

Notice that the spot on the paper gets very hot and may even catch fire!

What happens is that *all* the rays of the sun falling on the large lens are concentrated into a small point, which becomes very bright and hot. The heat is intense. Don't focus it on your skin! Think about the link between discarded glass bottles and forest fires.

Lenses have many uses besides using the sun's heat to make fire, and they make possible many important instruments. Let's look at some instruments which make use of lenses.

1   A microscope is used to examine ....very small objects..

2   It made possible the discovery of ..cells/bacteria/germs..

3   A telescope is used to observe ...large distant.. objects.

4   It made possible a detailed study of ...the heavens, stars and planets..

5   Spectacles or glasses are used to ...correct poor.. sight.

6   They enable many people to ...see clearly..

7   A camera is used to ...record visual information..

8   and make possible the ...recording.. of events, instead of relying on the painter.

Nowadays a great deal of use is made of lenses.

[9–13]
In this list underline those items which you think use lenses:

<u>photocopier</u>   <u>torch</u>   telephone   clock   television   <u>binoculars</u>
videorecorder   typewriter   <u>overhead projector</u>   computer   <u>camera</u>

The eye and vision

[14–22]
Although most lenses are made of glass, or more recently plastic, the eye uses a lens made of natural materials. Like many natural things it is, in many ways, better than an artificial lens.

Each of your eyes is shaped like a ball. Most of the eye is safely shielded inside your head.

At the front of the eye is a transparent outer layer called the **cornea**. This is the window to the eye.

The cornea is kept clean and healthy by constant washing with **tears** and wiping by the movement of the eyelids – blinking. If you get dust or grit in your eye, tears are made in an effort to wash it away.

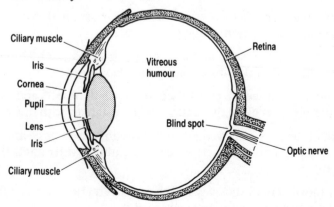

At the centre of the cornea is the coloured part of the eye, called the **iris**. Your iris may be blue or brown, or other shades – grey or green.

In the middle of the iris is an area which appears black. This is the **pupil**, and it is actually a hole which allows the light in.

The iris can contract or expand, making the pupil larger or smaller to control the amount of light entering the eye. The pupil is larger in low light and smaller in bright light. This is so we can see equally well in very bright light or when it is relatively dark. Notice how the size of your pupils changes in bright light and then dim light.

The light passing through the pupil is focused by the lens to form a sharp image on the **retina**.

Most **optical instruments**, like the microscope or the magnifying glass, focus sharp images by moving their lenses closer to or further from the eye.

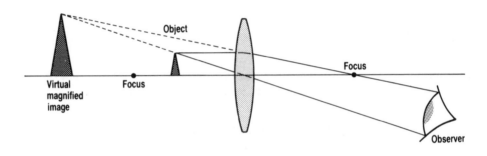

The eye focuses objects on the retina by changing the shape of the lens.

The retina is on the inside back wall of the eye and is composed of millions of light-sensitive cells. These convert the light falling on them in to electrical messages, which are sent to the brain through the **optic nerve**.

Every image that is focused on the retina is upside down, but the brain makes things appear the right way up.

We have two eyes set about 6–9 cm apart, so that each of them sees a slightly different view of the object that we are looking at.

Because of this we are able to see the depth of objects and to judge distances accurately. It is more difficult to judge distances with one eye closed.

Both of the eyes can swivel round through quite a large angle, using muscles to turn the eyeball. This allows us to see over a much larger angle than if the eyes were fixed.

The movement of the eyes and their coordination is controlled by the brain, without us being in the least aware of it.

14 How does the human eye focus on distant and close objects?

By changing the shape of the lens

15 What controls the amount of light reaching the retina? The iris, which makes the pupil smaller or larger

16 Why is it very important to protect the cornea from any damage or scratching? Scratches scatter light and so make the image blurred

17 What advantage do two eyes have over one? They enable us to judge distances and see the depth of objects

18 How does the focusing of the eye differ from that of a microscope or a camera? In the eye, the lens changes its shape. In the microscope or the camera, its position is changed

19 Why do we not see things upside down? We do but the brain corrects the image

20 What carries the information about what we see to the brain? The optic nerve

21 What is the purpose of the cornea? To protect the lens

22 How is the cornea kept clean and healthy? By tears and by blinking

Common faults of vision

[23–28]

A normal, healthy eye can see things sharply in focus whether they are 30 cm away or in the far distance. This happens because the lens is able to change its shape.

As a person gets older, the material of the lens gets stiffer and unable to change its shape so much. Thus older people cannot focus on objects over such a wide range, and find it harder to focus on close objects. It is normal even for people with good natural sight to need glasses for reading after the age of about 40.

With further ageing and more stiffening of the lens, several pairs of glasses may be needed to cover the full range of focus.

Short sight is called **myopia**. Many elderly people are myopic.

Some *young* people are longsighted and are unable to focus on close objects, while others are shortsighted and unable to see things sharply which are more than 30–60 cm distant.

In young people with long or short sight, the eyeball may not be quite round, or the lens may not have quite the correct range, or the cornea, which also affects the focus of the lens, may not quite suit the focusing of the lens.

The result is that in longsighted people the **image** of the object would be formed behind the retina. Long sight can be easily corrected with glasses, using a converging lens of the correct strength to bring objects into focus at the retina, rather than behind it.

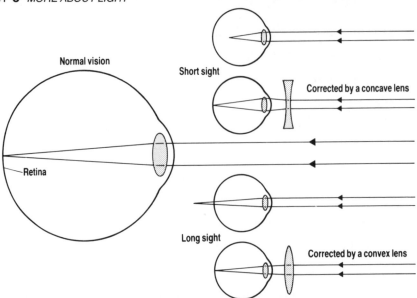

With short sight the image of the object is formed in front of the retina. This can be easily corrected by using glasses with diverging lenses of the correct strength to focus the image on the retina rather than in front of it.

23 What does a person with myopia suffer from? A stiffer lens which cannot focus over such a wide range

24 Why might an older person need several pairs of glasses to see all things well?

Older people's range of focus is limited, so they need several pairs of glasses to cover the full range

25 What kind of lens will a shortsighted person need?

A diverging lens/a concave lens

26 Why won't 'any old lens' of the right type do?

It needs to be of the correct strength

27–28 Suppose a young person has normal sight in the left eye and is longsighted in the right eye. What lenses will be needed to provide perfect sight? Left eye

plain glass Right eye converging lens

Absorption of light

[29–33]
Different materials affect light in various ways.

All things are made up of small units called **molecules**, which in turn are made up of two or more atoms.

If the molecules are relatively far apart, as they are in a gas such as air, light passes through without being seriously interrupted. These materials are **transparent**. This is also true of many liquids, such as water.

In solid substances, the molecules are more closely packed together and the light is more likely to bounce off molecules and be reflected.

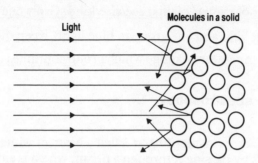

Many kinds of molecule do not reflect all the light which falls on them, but the atoms in the molecules collect or **absorb** *some* of the light. Only what is left is transmitted or reflected.

We have seen in *Science Progress Papers 1* that white light is actually composed of many colours. Atoms are only able to absorb light of a particular colour and so materials containing molecules made up from these atoms appear coloured.

29–30 All substances are made up of .molecules.. which themselves contain several .atoms..

31 Are molecules packed more closely in liquids than in solids? ..No..

32 What light gets reflected from a coloured solid?
.The light which was not absorbed...

33 What do you think happens to light in a coloured liquid? .Light which is not.. .absorbed passes through – is transmitted.

[34–41]
Leaves which are illuminated by white light appear green.

34 What colour will the leaves reflect? .Green..

35–36 What colours are absorbed by the atoms and molecules of the leaves?
.Blue.. and .red..

All leaves contain a green pigment called **chlorophyll**. This pigment uses the energy from sunlight to produce the food necessary for the plant to grow. The process of changing light energy into plant food is called **photosynthesis**.

Even red and yellow leaves contain chlorophyll although its colour is masked by the other colours.

37 Underline the colours of light you would expect to be most effective in making a green plant grow.

<u>blue</u> green <u>red</u>

38–41 Can you suggest an experiment which would prove that this is so?

Grow up a number of similar plants: age/size/kind. Grow one group in red light,

one group in green light and one group in blue light. Keep them equally watered

and at the same temperature – judge which group continues to grow best

The spectrum and spectroscopy

[42–49]

We have learnt in *Science Progress Papers 1* that a beam of white light can be split up into its many colours by passing it through a prism, which is a triangular block of glass.

The 'rainbow' of light which is produced by the prism is called a **spectrum**. All the colours making up the original beam of light are visible separately.

When a substance is heated hot enough it produces or **emits** light. For example, when an iron nail is held in a flame it glows red hot, and if the flame is hot enough it glows almost white.

When a substance is heated, energy is given to it. This energy makes the atoms in the substance much more active or **excited**. The excited atoms need to get rid of this excess energy, and they give out, or emit, light.

Remember, light is a form of energy.

Each kind of atom emits light of a particular colour when it is heated. If copper is heated in a flame it gives a characteristic blue colour, while salt, which contains sodium atoms, gives a yellow colour.

If we use a prism to produce a spectrum from the light emitted from a heated substance we will see that the spectrum consists of several narrow bands of colour and the rest of the spectrum is dark.

This kind of spectrum is called an **emission spectrum**.

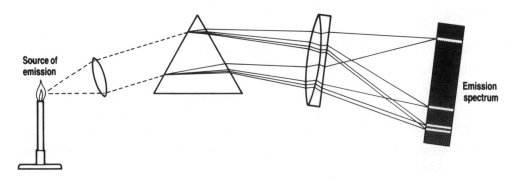

Source of emission

Emission spectrum

This emission spectrum can be examined using an instrument called a **spectroscope**. Each substance gives a unique pattern.

A spectroscope can be used to examine the light coming from the sun or stars. This gives scientists a great deal of information about what sorts of atom there are in the sun or stars, without needing to visit them!

42 What is a spectrum? ...Light split into its component colours by a prism..

43 Why does a heated substance produce light? ...The atoms are 'excited' and give off.. ..energy...

44 What is special about the light produced by heating a particular atom?

....It has a characteristic colour

45 What can scientists use a spectroscope for?

...To gain information about the atoms that are present in hot objects.

State whether the following are true or false:

46 All flames produce the same colours. ..False...

47 A glass prism splits up light into its component colours. ...True...

48 A spectroscope could be used to find out whether any tin cans were burning on a bonfire. ...True..

49 A spectroscope could be used to find out what atoms were present in a particular sample of a mixed metal like steel (which is made up of atoms of iron and other substances). ...True..

The camera

[50–54]
The camera is probably the most familiar optical instrument.

We described how you could make a pinhole camera in *Science Progress Papers 1*. The biggest problem with the pinhole camera is that the sharpness of focus depends on the size of the pin hole. The smaller the hole the sharper the image is, but at the same time a very small hole restricts the amount of light getting in and the image produced is dim.

This problem can be overcome by using a lens to focus the image.

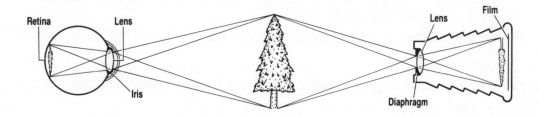

The image is focused accurately on the surface of the film by moving the lens backward or forward on a screw thread.

The amount of light which enters the camera, and thus the brightness of the image formed on the film , is controlled by the **iris diaphragm**. This is really a hole whose size can be varied.

The image only needs to fall on the film for a very short time. This is controlled by the **shutter**, which is a blind which covers the hole where the light enters. It moves away for a brief period to **expose** the film.

50–52　What features does the camera have in common with the eye? .A.lens... and

　　　　.an iris... and .film/retina to receive the image...

53　What works in a different way in the camera compared with the eye? ..The.lens...

54　What has a similar function in the camera to the retina of the eye? ..The.film...

Photographic film

[55–59]
The film records the image which the camera 'sees'.

It is a flexible transparent plastic sheet with a thin layer of a special coating, or **emulsion**, on one side.

This emulsion is made up of very fine grains of a substance that contains silver distributed, or **dispersed**, in a layer of gelatin. The gelatin is similar to the material used for making jellies.

Certain silver-containing substances are sensitive to light. The light is absorbed by the atoms of silver, which are changed in such a way that, when the film is **developed**, the grains of silver turn black.

When a black-and-white film is exposed in a camera and the film is subsequently developed, it shows up black where light fell on it and remains transparent everywhere else. So it shows the image in reverse – black where it was light and clear where it was dark. It is a **negative**.

A **positive print** can then be produced by shining a light through the negative onto another piece of photographic emulsion, this time coated on paper.

When this paper is developed, an image will be produced the right way round, with black where the image was dark and light where the image was light. This is a black-and-white photograph.

55　What in the photographic film changes when it absorbs light?

　　.The atoms of silver...

56　Why is the first image produced a negative one? .Because the light makes silver..

　　.go black when it is developed..

57 How can a print resembling the original scene be produced? .By .shining .light...
.through .the negative onto another piece of photographic emulsion....

58 What is the purpose of the gelatin in a photographic film? .To .hold .the .grains .of....
....silver .substance .in .a .distributed .way..

59 What has to be done to the film after it has been exposed in the camera?
...It .has .to .be .developed..

Moving pictures

[60–69]
Fill in the blanks from the list below:

retains   moving   separate   faded   drawing
series   illusion continuous changed   different

We have all been to the cinema and seen .moving... pictures where almost perfect

movement is recorded. How is this illusion.... of movement obtained?

Get an old note-book or diary and then in the top right-hand corner make a little

.drawing.... on each page. Each drawing should be in about the same place and

should be a little .different... from the previous one.

This picture should give you an idea.

Then flick through the pages with your left-hand thumb. Notice how the pictures
appear to show smooth, continuous movement.

This is rather like a movie film or a television picture.

In both cases, the pictures are actually shown as a series.... of still pictures, but as

long as the pictures are .changed.... about 25 times in a second, the eye will not

see the separate..... images but will see the changes as smooth, ..continuous...
movement.

This is because of the **persistence of vision** of the eye. The eye retains.... the image
that it sees for about 0.1 of a second after the image ceases; for example, after you
turn off the light or close your eyes.

In this way, each picture on the movie screen or television set is presented to the

eye before the previous image has faded....

Beats and discords

[1–5]

When two tuning forks or bells of the same pitch are sounded together, their notes blend and strengthen each other.

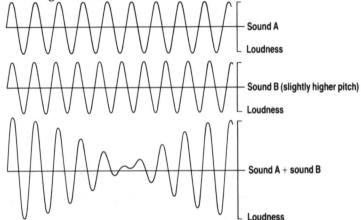

Sound A
Loudness

Sound B (slightly higher pitch)
Loudness

Sound A + sound B
Loudness

If they do not produce exactly the same pitch, the sounds that they produce will swell and fade at regular intervals. These variations of loudness are called **beats** and occur because the vibrations of the two are 'out of step' with each other.

If one bell vibrates 256 times a second and the second bell 257 times a second, the two bells sounded together will produce a beat every second.

Most people do not notice beats of less than 5 or 6 per second, but if the number of beats increases to about 30 per second the sound becomes very unpleasant to listen to. We call it a **dissonance** or discord.

As the number of beats increases above 40 beats per second the ear no longer hears the separate beats and the unpleasant sensation disappears.

1 Why do the instruments in a band need to be tuned to produce the same pitch?

..To avoid beats and discords..

2 How closely do they need to be tuned? ..Closer than a difference of about five..

..cycles per second..

3 What sort of sound do badly tuned instruments make? ..Discord..

4 If one bell had a pitch of 512 cycles per second and another bell a pitch of 482 cycles per second, would you expect to be disturbed by the sound of them both ringing

together? ..Yes..

5 If the second bell was filed down so that it now vibrated at 506 cycles per second, would you expect to find the sound of them both ringing together acceptable?

..Yes/just

Noise

[6–18]
Fill in the missing words from this list:

accidents   damage   loud   environment   concentrate   powerful   deaf
irritating   unpleasant   repetitive   discos   pollutants   persistent

Sounds can be pleasing or they can be ..unpleasant.. Some sounds are found

..irritating.. and displeasing by some people, while others enjoy them. In general,

..repetitive.. or extremely ..loud.. sounds are usually unpleasant to most people
and are called **noise**.

Intensely loud noise can actually harm people and ..damage.. their hearing.
Boilermakers, riveters and steelworkers who have worked for a long time in an

extremely noisy ..environment.. often become quite ..deaf..

The use of excessively ..powerful.. amplifiers at ..discos.. can cause deafness,
especially among the fans of 'heavy metal' pop music, because it is particularly
loud.

A noise does not have to be very loud to cause people to become tired or irritable, if
it is continuous or periodic. The steady whine of a power saw or even the

..persistent.. dripping of a tap can be very distressing to the sufferer.

Your brain cannot ..concentrate.. properly if you are hearing continuous noise. This
is a danger to drivers, pilots and people working heavy machines, because it can

cause ..accidents..

In scientific terms we can define or describe noise as a sound with no regular
pattern to it.

Noise is one of the most common and least controlled ..pollutants.. of the modern
city.

[19–30]
Look carefully at this picture:

Name six objects or activities which are making this environment uncomfortably noisy, and for each one give an idea for making its noise more acceptable.

19–20   ..Noisy motorbike.. could be reduced by ..driving it more reasonably/having a.. ..better silencer fitted..

21–22   .Rolling barrels... could be reduced by ..carrying them..

23–24   .Transistor stereo.. could be reduced by ..using it at reduced volume..

25–26   .Pneumatic drill.. could be reduced by ..operating it with a muffler..

27–28   .Jet airliner... could be reduced by ..flying higher or siting landing fields away.. ..from centres of population..

29–30   .People shouting.. could be reduced by ..speaking at normal levels..

Hearing

[31–38]
Hearing is an essential sense. Without it we would be living in a world of silence, out of touch with much that goes on around us. Next time you ride a bicycle in traffic, notice how much you learn of what is going on behind you through your hearing.

The construction of the ear enables it to catch sound waves that come to it through the air.

The waves enter the ear and travel through a tube to the eardrum, which is a membrane which vibrates or quivers as the sound waves hit it.

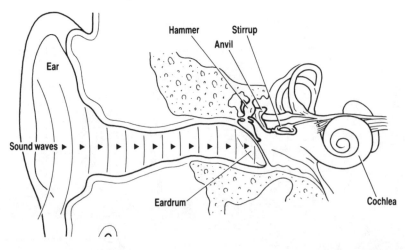

Inside the eardrum and protected by it are three tiny bones which are called the **hammer, anvil** and **stirrup**, because of their shapes.

These bones are thought to increase or amplify the sound and convey it to the **cochlea**. The cochlea is shaped rather like a snail shell. It is filled with fluid and contains a very large number of tiny hairs which are attached to nerves.

As the sound waves travel through the fluid they vibrate these tiny hairs and the movement is detected by the nerves. They pass the information to the brain.

Some sounds do not vibrate with enough energy to make the eardrum vibrate, and they cannot be heard. They are said to be below the **threshold of audibility**. (A threshold is an entrance, a gateway or a starting point.)

Some sounds are so loud that they hurt the ear. These are above the **threshold of feeling**.

Some animals have hearing which is much more **acute** than that of human beings.

Generally, the human ear can only hear sounds which vibrate faster than about 30 times a second and slower than about 14 000 times a second. By the age of 45 the ability to hear high-pitched sounds decreases until vibrations faster than 8000 times a second become inaudible.

Many children can hear the high-pitched squeaks made by bats, but few adults can.

Many animals are much more sensitive to high sounds and some can hear vibrations of 40 000 times a second.

Underline your answer to question 31 from the answers in brackets.

31   Most animals have two ears (because two are more sensitive than one, <u>to tell the direction of sounds</u>, in case one ear fails).

32   Why does the human outer ear have its curious cup-like shape? ....To.direct.the. ...sound.into.the.ear.

33   Cats are constantly swivelling their ears. Why is this? ...To.gather.in.the.sounds.. .better.

34   Why can we not hear a dog-whistle when dogs can? ....The.human.ear.cannot. ....perceive.the.very.high-pitched.sounds

35   If you fail to hear a whisper it will be because it is ...below.the.threshold.of. ...audibility.

36   What does the eardrum do? ...Protects.the.inner.ear.while.passing.on.the.sound.

37   What do the hammer, anvil and stirrup contribute to hearing? ...They.transfer.. ....and.amplify.the.sound.from.the.eardrum.to.the.cochlea

38   Sound waves are converted to nerve impulses in the ...cochlea.

Perception of sound

[39–45]

Humans have lost some of the acute hearing that most wild animals possess, but we can still use our perception of sound to make us aware of what is going on around us.

We have two ears, as we have two eyes, and this helps us to detect accurately where a sound comes from. Try resting your head on one side on your desk. Notice how sounds seem to be more diffuse, and how your awareness of the position of sound in space is weakened.

The brain plays a big part in hearing. It enables us to sort out sounds. If you are listening to music, notice how you can concentrate on part of the music, for example the deep notes, and largely ignore the rest.

Similarly, if you concentrate hard you can hear what someone is saying against a considerable amount of background noise.

The brain also makes it possible to perceive the direction of sounds.

The sound from a particular source arrives at each of our ears at a slightly different time and by a slightly different path.

For example, a sound occurring on our left-hand side will have to travel a shorter distance to the left ear and will arrive a little sooner.

The brain can interpret these small time differences between hearing in each ear, and work out where the sound comes from.

We *hear* sounds with our ears, but our brains can select from these sounds and calculate the direction of one sound out of many.

It is the brain which adds so much to our *perception* of sound and makes it possible to detect the position of an aeroplane in the sky, even when there is a good deal of other noise.

If we turn our heads, the brain is able to recalculate the direction of the sound.

Underline your answer to question 39 from the answers in brackets.

39   We have two ears (in case one fails, <u>to provide the brain with more information</u> , to make the head look balanced).

State whether the following are true or false:

40   The brain helps us to select particular sounds out of many. ..True...

41   A person who is deaf in one ear can easily tell where sounds come from. .False....

42   Detecting where a sound comes from depends on keeping still. ..False..

43   Humans have a keener perception of sound than other animals. ..False...

44   A very noisy environment makes the perception of sound more difficult. ..True..

45   If you are very distracted, your perception of sound will be less good. ...True..

Speech

[46–54]
Humans are the only animals to use complex language and to produce a large range of clearly distinguishable sounds, which make up the spoken word.

The range of sounds which the human voice can produce is made in the voice box or **larynx**.

This is located between the back of the tongue and the windpipe or **trachea**. Every breath of air that passes in or out of the lungs passes through the larynx.

The larynx is box-shaped and is kept in this shape by sections of bluish-white, rubbery stuff called **cartilage**. Gristle that you often find in meat is cartilage – you can see it in the breastbone of many chickens.

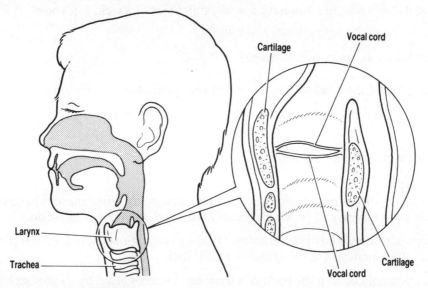

Sound is produced within the box by the **vocal cords**. The vocal cords are two bands of elastic tissue which are stretched or altered in shape and brought close together by small muscles.

When the vocal cords are brought close together, the air rushing between them produces sound. The shape and stretch of the vocal cords determines the pitch of the sound. The loudness of the sound depends on the rush of air through the vocal cords.

You can perhaps understand this better by an experiment with a balloon. Blow up the balloon and stretch its neck sideways. As the air rushes out it makes a wailing noise, which varies in pitch as you stretch or slacken the neck.

The sound made in the larynx has to travel through the throat and mouth before reaching the outside.

So the **quality** of the voice depends on the shape of a person's throat, nose and mouth, as well as the control of the breathing used to produce it.

The sounds produced are also influenced by how sharply the sound is started and how suddenly it is cut off. The lips and tongue play a big part in this, while the shape of the lips affects the nature of the sound.

So the larynx, the tongue and the lips all work together to produce the rich and varied sounds which make up human speech. Speech provides complex communication not only with words and sentences, but also with tone of voice. Think how the meaning of a phrase can be altered by the way it is said. For example, 'It is time for *tea*' or 'It is *time* for tea'.

46 What controls the pitch of a sound that you make? The shape and stretch of the vocal cords

47 What controls the loudness of the sound? The rush of air through the vocal cords

48 What decides whether you have a weak, thin voice or a rich, full voice? The shape of the nose, throat and mouth

49 What keeps the voice box in shape? Cartilage

50–54 What parts of the head do you use when you speak, besides the brain? Vocal cords and throat and nose and mouth and tongue

How animals make sounds

[55–60]

Lions roar, birds sing, donkeys bray. These and many other animals have vocal cords and a larynx and produce sounds in much the same way as we do.

They use these sounds for communication – to attract mates, to frighten prey, to warn other members of the group or to call their young.

Have you noticed that the bleat of a lamb can be recognised by its mother? There must be more variation in these apparently similar sounds than we can hear.

In recent years, scientists have realised that whales emit a large variety of sounds which carry long distances under water. It is believed that some of these sounds work rather like an echo sounder (see *Science Progress Papers 1*), but other patterns of sound appear to be communication with other whales.

Bats emit an extremely high-pitched twittering, often too high for the human ear to hear. These very high-pitched, or **ultrasonic**, sounds are echoed back off solid objects like the walls of caves. The bat's acute hearing enables it to 'see' where it is going in the dark, at least as well as our eyes would in the light.

Other animals make sounds in quite different ways.

The cricket or grasshopper rubs the surfaces of its wings and legs together very rapidly to make its chirping sound.

The buzzing of flies, bees and many other insects is caused by the vibrations of their wings as they beat rapidly against the air.

55–56 Whales use sound to <u>communicate</u> as well as <u>navigate</u>

57 What are ultrasonic sounds? <u>Very high-pitched sounds; too high for human ears</u> <u>to hear</u>

58 Do all sheep make exactly similar sounds? <u>No</u>

59 Why do birds have a whole range of song? <u>To communicate different things –</u> <u>attract a mate, warn others etc.</u>

60 Why do you think that lions roar? <u>To frighten their prey</u>

PAPER 5 UNDERSTANDING AND MAKING USE OF ELECTRICITY

The electric cell was discovered in the nineteenth century. Groups of cells or **batteries** made a convenient source of electrical power.

Using these batteries, many of the rules or laws of electricity were discovered, but it was not until scientists began to understand atoms that anyone could explain how electricity worked.

When Sir J.J. Thompson discovered the **electron**, scientists were able to explain how electricity flowed like water.

[1–15]

It helps to understand the flow of electricity if you imagine the battery as a tank of water, which is connected to a water wheel through a pipe with a tap.

This behaves in a very similar way to an electrical circuit.

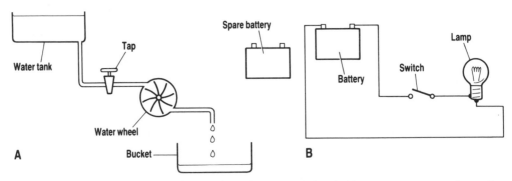

The water wheel **resists** turning and so the water wheel takes some energy from the flow of water and reduces its flow.

If we raise the tank, the water will run more rapidly through the pipe and the wheel will run faster.

By raising the tank we have increased the pressure of the water.

1   What is the electrical equivalent to the tank of water in B? ...The battery...

2   How can we increase the flow of electricity in B? ..Adding more batteries..

3   What would happen to the bulb? ...It would become brighter.

4   How can we stop the water wheel? ..By turning off the tap...

5   What in diagram B is equivalent to the tap? ...The switch.

6   Suppose we replaced the pipe in A with a very narrow pipe. What do you think would happen to the water wheel? ...It would turn more slowly.

7   Suppose we replaced the wire to the lamp in B with a very fine piece of wire. What do you think might happen to the lamp? ..It would become dimmer..

Raising the level of water in the tank increases the pressure.

To increase the electrical pressure you can raise the **voltage** by adding further batteries.

So voltage ~~is~~ a measure of the *pressure* of the electricity. It is measured in **volts**. (They are called after Count Volta, who invented the first practical battery.)

8 Suppose the tank is at a fixed height above the water wheel. In what two ways could you control the rate at which water flows and the wheel turns? ...By partially.. ..closing the tap and by using narrow pipes.

So the rate that water flows depends on how the pipe or the wheel resists the flow.

9 In diagram B, with the same number of batteries, what will control the brightness of the lamp? ....The resistance of the wires or the lamp.

10–11 The rate that electricity flows in B depends on the **resistance** of the ..wires.. or the ..lamp..

The *rate of flow* of electricity – the electric **current** – is measured in **amps**. (They are named after Ampère, who made major discoveries about electrical currents.)

12–13 If we leave the tap open for very long, what will happen to the tank? ..It will run dry.. and the wheel will ..stop...

14–15 If we leave circuit B switched on for some time, what will happen to the batteries? ....They will go dead.. and the lamp will ..go out..

Batteries, like the water tank, have a limited **capacity**. How long they last depends on how fast electricity is taken from them – how great a current is drawn.

[16–20]
Let's compare electricity and water a little further.

16 Suppose we have two wheels and the water flows first through one and then through the other. Will they turn as fast as when there was only one? ..No..

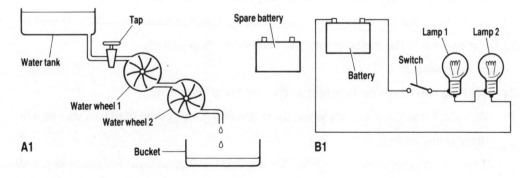

A1   Water tank   Tap   Water wheel 1   Water wheel 2   Bucket   Spare battery   Battery   Switch   Lamp 1   Lamp 2   B1

17 How much water will flow when there are two wheels compared with when there is only the single one? ..The.same.amount....

18 How long does all the water take to run out of the tank when there are two wheels compared with when there is only one? ...The.same.time.(or.longer.if.the.wheels. ...resist.the.flow.strongly.)..

In diagram B1:

19 Will each of the two lamps be as bright as the one was? .No....

20 Will the battery last as long when there are two lamps connected this way as when there is one? ..Yes.(or.longer.)...

In this circuit the lamps are connected after one another. We say that the connections are made in **series**.

[21–25]
Now let's connect them rather differently.

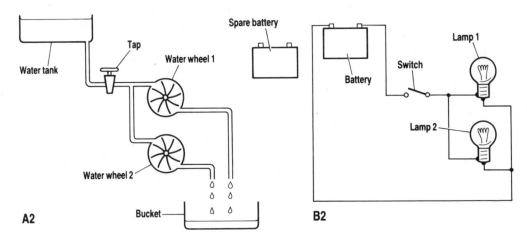

A2   B2

In diagram A2:

21 Will the two wheels now turn as rapidly as one alone does? .Yes....

22 How much water will now flow compared with just one wheel? .Twice.as.much...

23 How long will the water in the tank last now? ..Half.as.long..

In diagram B2:

24 Will the two lamps be as bright as the one lamp was? .Yes....

25 Will the battery last as long when there are two lamps connected this way as when there is one lamp? .No....

The connections are side by side. We say that the connections are made in **parallel**.

[26–27]

From the last set of diagrams, show in drawings how you would connect a second battery to the first one in the circuit to do each of the following things:

26 Make the lamps shine longer.

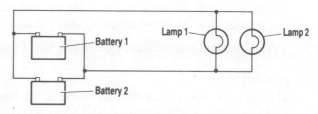

27 Make the lamps shine brighter.

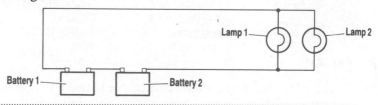

In the examples we have just been considering, water flows from the tank pushing water along the pipe. This in turn pushes water out of the end of the pipe.

This is rather like a tube full of marbles – pushing one marble into one end will cause one marble to be pushed out of the other end.

Electricity behaves in much the same way. The battery produces electrons which push out electrons in the first atoms of the wire. These electrons go on to the next atoms, and so on down the wire. We call this **conduction** – electricity is **conducted**.

The material the electricity flows through is called a **conductor**. Not all materials will exchange electrons equally easily to allow a flow of electric current, and so there are good conductors and bad conductors of electricity.

Generally metals are good conductors; copper, silver, gold and aluminium are among the best. We can use copper to make high-quality wire.

Glass, wood and plastics are poor conductors and are known as **insulators**. We can insulate electrical wires with plastics.

Some materials conduct electricity moderately well – they allow electrons to flow but offer quite a bit of resistance to the flow, rather like the narrow pipe with water that we looked at earlier. These materials are often called **resistors**.

The resistance which they offer takes energy out of the electric current. They heat up as the current flows.

Even good conductors offer *some* resistance to flow, and if they are very thin compared with the amount of current they carry they will heat up. If the current is large and their surface area is small, so that they can't pass on the heat to the air as fast as it is produced, they will get hotter and hotter until they melt or burn.

Metals can be used in this way to act as **fuses**. They are arranged to melt through and break the circuit when the current becomes too high. Fuses are used to protect electrical devices from damage if the device goes wrong so that there is a sudden surge of current. If a fuse melts or **blows**, something is almost always wrong with the circuit. It must be switched off and the fault found before the fuse is replaced.

Pure water will not conduct electricity, but if salts are dissolved in the water it will.

[28–39]
Here is a list of electrical devices found in the home. Put a ring around the ones which you think will use the resistance of a conductor to produce heat deliberately. Underline those that produce heat incidentally, as they do other work.

electric kettle   electric drill   television set   incandescent lamp
torch   electric cooker   radio   telephone
washing machine   refrigerator   doorbell   vacuum cleaner

[40–44]

40 Which of the following would be suitable to make the connections? Underline the answer(s). (String, cotton, <u>copper wire, aluminium foil</u>)

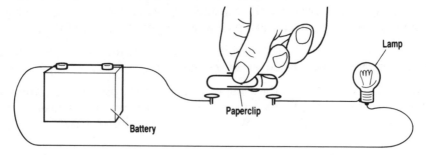

Battery   Paperclip   Lamp

Would the lamp light if the drawing pins were bridged with:

41 a strip of paper? ..No..

42 a metal paperclip? ..Yes..

43 a piece of glass? ..No..

44 a piece of string soaked with salty water? ..Yes..

Electromagnetism

[45–52]
Fill in the missing words from this list:

iron   flow   messages   magnet   telegraph   magnetic   current   switch

We saw in *Science Progress Papers 1* that Ampère and Faraday showed that an

electric ..current.. flowing in a wire caused the wire to act like a weak magnet, and

that moving a ..magnet.. in and out of a coil of wire made an electric current ..flow..

They then found that when a coil of wire carrying a current was wound round a piece of iron, the ..iron... behaved like a strong magnet. They had discovered the **electromagnet** or **solenoid**.

This led directly to the invention of the **relay**.

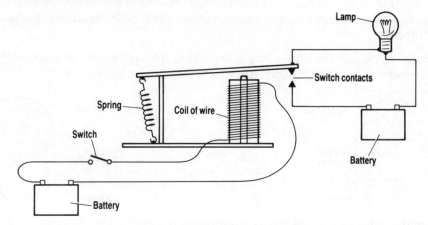

When the ..switch... is closed a current flows through the coil of wire. This turns the iron **core** into a magnet. It then attracts the iron bar which closes the switch contacts. When the current is switched off, the iron core ceases to be ..magnetic.. and the bar is released and pulled back by the spring, and the switch contacts open. In a slightly different arrangement the bar can be used to punch a hole in a paper strip, or to pull a pen against a moving strip of paper. ..Messages.. were sent for many years using this arrangement, which was the basis of the electric ..telegraph..

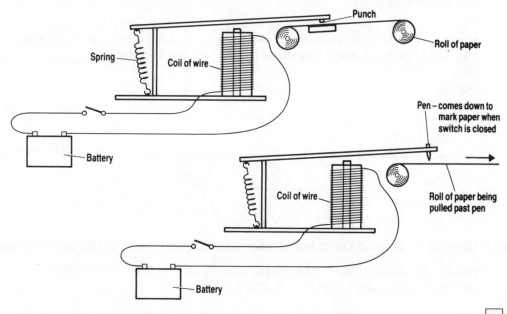

[53–55]

It was then realised that if a sheet of suitable material was used to collect sound waves, and this sheet was attached to a magnet in a coil, an electric current would be caused to flow.

The strength of the current depended on the amount of movement, which in turn depended on the strength of the sound waves – the louder the sound, the greater the current.

A similar device, in the same circuit, converted the varying electric current back into sound waves – the stronger the current, the louder the sound.

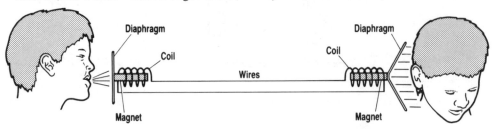

53 The device which collected the sound waves was called a .microphone..

54 The device which produced the sound waves from the electric current was called

   .a loudspeaker/earpiece/headphone.

55 The combination of the two devices with long wires linking them makes a

   .telephone.

[56–61]

When sound is recorded for a tape, the varying electric currents that the microphone produces are used in a tape recorder to magnetise a strip of magnetic tape permanently.

When the tape is played back, by moving it past a coil of wire, the varying magnetism of the tape is converted back into an electric current. This current is converted into mechanical vibrations by a device like a loudspeaker.

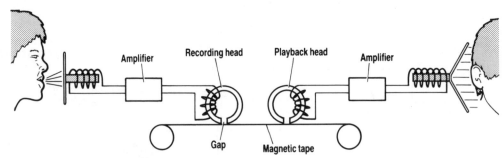

56–61 Here is a list of electrical gadgets. Underline the ones which use electromagnetism.

   radio   telephone   fan   cassette player   lamp   kettle   record player
   computer disc drive   cooker   hotplate

Electric motors and generators

[62–64]

These two devices, which are so important to our modern lifestyle, are really very similar. An electric motor can be turned to generate electricity; an electric current passed through a generator will make it turn like a motor.

When practical motors and generators, or **dynamos**, were first developed, it was more convenient to move the coil of wire and to keep the magnet stationary.

To supply the current to the rotating coil in the case of the motor, or to collect the current produced in the case of the dynamo, a special arrangement is necessary. This is called a **commutator**.

The commutator consists of a copper ring which is cut into sections. The ends of the coil, or coils, are soldered to opposite segments and pieces of carbon press against these segments to supply or collect the current.

These pieces of carbon are called **brushes**. Carbon is a very good brush material because it conducts electricity, wears slowly and smoothly and, being softer than copper, does not wear out the copper commutator.

More powerful motors or generators use more than one rotating coil and often use an electromagnet instead of the permanent magnet.

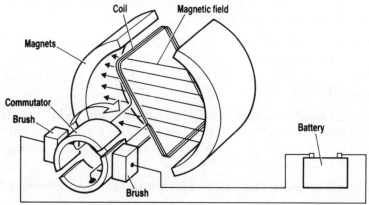

62 What function does the commutator have? To supply the current to the rotating coil, or collect the current from it

63 What will wear out first in an electric motor? The brushes

64 Why do some motors have more than one rotating coil? To give them more power

[65–67]

65 **Water** is to **electricity** as **water molecules** are to electrons

66 **Water** is to **electricity** as **pipe** is to wire

67 **Tap** is to **switch** as water is to **electricity**.

[68–74]

When a tap is opened and water runs out of a tank, the time taken to empty the tank will depend on how big the tank is and how fast the water flows out.

Similarly the time taken for a battery to run out will depend on how big it is and how fast the electric current flows out of it.

The power taken by an electrical device such as a lamp or electric motor can be measured by the voltage connected to it, and by the electric current which passes through it.

So if we have a torch with a 6 volt battery and the bulb takes 0.5 amp of current, we say that the power of the bulb is 3 **watts**.

Power is measured in **watts = volts × amps**.

68   A toy electric train which uses 12 volts to drive it uses 1 amp of current. What is the power of the motor? ...12.. watts.

The electricity supply that is normally provided to the home in the UK is 240 volts and most of the electrical gadgets we have at home are designed to work best with this voltage.

The power that these things take is usually marked on them. For example, a typical electric light bulb takes 100 watts, an electric kettle 2000 watts, a television set 200 watts and a small clock radio maybe only 10 watts.

REMEMBER THAT VOLTAGES WHICH ARE MORE THAN ABOUT 100 VOLTS ARE DANGEROUS AND CAN GIVE ELECTRIC SHOCKS – THE ELECTRICITY SUPPLY IS *240* VOLTS AND CAN CAUSE FATAL ELECTRIC SHOCK.

We are charged for electricity in units of a kilowatt-hour. (A kilowatt is 1000 watts.) This means that 1000 watts used for one hour will cost one unit, which at present may be as much as 6–9 pence. So we can easily see that leaving a 100 watt light on for 10 hours will cost us 6–9 pence.

69   How long could we use a small clock radio for the same cost as using a 100 watt light for 2 hours? ...20.hours.

70–71   Here is a list of electrical appliances with their typical power consumption:

toaster 1000 watts   kettle 2500 watts   iron 1000 watts
refrigerator 180 watts   television 250 watts   radio 12 watts   or
electric lamps 150 watts) vacuum 600 watts   food mixer 380 watts
each

Draw a ring around the one you think is likely to contribute most to the weekly electricity bill and underline the one you think will cost least. *Think about how long they get used*, as well as their power consumption.

72   Is the electricity bill likely to be bigger/smaller/about the same in the winter?

...Bigger.

73   Why should this be so?   <u>The lights are used for much longer</u>

74   How can a high electricity bill be most easily reduced by good management?

<u>By turning off all unnecessary lights and the television when not needed</u>

For all its grand-sounding name, information technology is almost as old as the human race.

[1–2]
Long before written languages, our ancestors had learnt to communicate vital information by such means as scratching drawings and primitive maps on stones and the walls of caves. These passed on to others the whereabouts of good hunting.

1 Was this information available to many people? ..No..

2 Why was it not convenient? ..People had to visit the cave or stones to get the.. ..information..

The invention of writing, first on clay tablets and then on paper, made it possible to keep extensive records. But each copy of each record had to be written by hand. This took an immense amount of time.

The invention of printing

[3–4]
The printing press with movable type was invented by a German printer, Johann Gutenburg, in the fifteenth century. After that many copies of books and records could be produced rapidly and circulated widely.

3 How could information in books be circulated widely?

By transporting the books by horse-drawn vehicles or by hand..

4 What limited the speed of this method of communication?

.The speed or distance people or horses could travel

Early military communications

[5–8]
Wars have always put pressure on inventiveness. One thing they needed was communication between distant parts of the army or between fighting ships at sea.

In a battle it was important to exchange messages rapidly. Bugles and special bugle calls were used to send simple messages on land. Their sound carried for considerable distances.

5 What do you think would limit communication by these means?

The distance that sounds would carry, and the noises of battle

At sea, where visibility was good and unhindered by trees and hills, messages were sent by flag signals.

Rows of specially patterned flags hung from a ship's yardarm could be seen from much greater distances, particularly with telescopes. They could communicate relatively long messages.

Messages on land and sea were also signalled by waving two flags in a special order. This became known as **semaphore**. It was extended by building large towers with two long arms which could be raised and lowered as if they were signalling flags, but could be seen much further.

Underline your answer to question 6 from the list that follows it.

6 How far do you think messages could be exchanged by semaphore, even using telescopes and under favourable conditions?

150 km   15 km   1.5 km   Less than 1.5 km

7 Would communication by flags or semaphore be affected by the weather? Yes

8 Would the time of day greatly affect flag or semaphore communication?

Yes – no communication in darkness

[9–10]
Another way of signalling information from one place to another was the **heliograph**. This used a mirror of glass or polished metal to reflect the rays of the sun to the person receiving.

Have you ever noticed how far the sun's rays can be seen reflected in a car's windscreen?

9 Can you suggest any way in which flashes of light reflected from a mirror could be used to send understandable messages? By flashing the light according to a code

10 How would this method of communication be restricted by the weather?

It depends on the sun

[11–12]

At the time of the Spanish Armada a system was set up to send a simple message rapidly over the length and breadth of England. It took a lot of organisation.

The message was the warning that the Armada had been sighted.

A chain of bonfires was built on high ground, with each bonfire in sight of the one before it. As the Armada was sighted the first bonfire was lit. When it flared and became visible to the next one, that was lit, and so the message went down the chain until all of England knew.

Each bonfire **relayed** the news in turn.

The people knew the nature of the expected message so the signal only had to carry simple information. No fire meant 'No! not yet'.

11   The lit bonfires meant '..Yes..!, now'.

12   What is meant by a relay station? ...A station which receives the message and..

..repeats it for a further distance..

So we see one of the first uses of the simple message; no signal means no and a signal means yes. This principle is used in many modern machines.

The electric telegraph and telephone

[13–14]

In the nineteenth century, it was shown that an electric current would deflect a compass needle. The current could be turned on and off with a switch, and the needle would indicate the position of the switch.

It was also shown that these electric currents could travel along very long lengths of wire, so that you could control a needle from far away.

A new means of communication became possible. People used the switch to turn the current on and off, and read the message by observing the movement of a compass needle at the other end.

This was the **electric telegraph**. Extremely long distances could be covered by using relay stations, which received the message and passed it on.

13   What limitation did the early electric telegraph have in common with the

heliograph? ..Messages needed to be sent in some sort of code..

14   Where else do we find the idea of relay stations for carrying messages?

..The Armada bonfires..

[15–20]

Fill in the missing words from the list below:

lamps   code   signals   communciation   telegraph   letters

The electric ..telegraph.. provided almost instant ..communication.. between distant points.

Before it could be really useful it was essential to devise a ...code... to convert the on/off of an electric current into ..letters..

The first successful code was the Morse Code, which used two different 'on' periods, one long and one short.

These long and short ..signals.. were used in different combinations to spell out words.

For example: a short signal followed by a long one represented A; one short = B; two shorts = I; three shorts = S, and so on.

The Morse Code could not only be used with the electric telegraph but also with signalling ..lamps.. and even the heliograph.

With the discovery of radio, messages could be sent even further using Morse Code.

[21–24]
With an increasing understanding of electromagnetism, scientists were able to vary an electric current, rather than just switch it on or off.

They soon devised a means of doing this according to the amount and quality of the sound which reached a lightweight disc or **diaphragm**.

Underline your answers to questions 21–22 from the words in brackets.

21 This device was called a (megaphone, earphone, microphone).

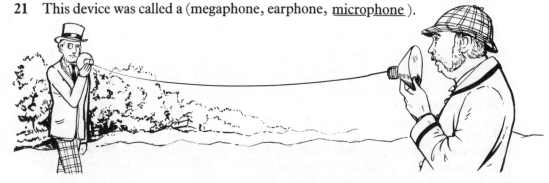

Similarly, they invented a means of turning the varying electric current back into sound.

22 These two inventions, together, produced the (television, telephone, telegraph, radar) .

23–24 They made possible the transmission of ..speech.. directly by ..wire.. and made it possible for two people to communicate over considerable distances by talking directly.

This reduced the need for expert signallers (telegraphists) who were employed to send and read the messages in Morse Code.

It was also much faster, so that important business transactions could now be carried out quickly and easily. World trade benefited greatly.

The typewriter

[25–29]
Written records were still important for storing information for long-term reference. Until after 1900 details of most transactions were still handwritten, employing a whole army of clerks to write everything down laboriously.

During the eighteenth and nineteenth centuries many inventors had attempted to make a practicable typewriter. It had to be fast and easy to use as well as being relatively cheap.

It was not until after 1874 that the first satisfactory machine appeared. It used a set of keys, one for each letter, linked by a set of levers driving a piece of type to strike the paper.

As soon as cheap and reliable machines became generally available, they replaced the mass of clerks in offices and the new skill of typing became important.

With carbon paper placed between the sheets of typing paper, the typewriter could produce several copies of a letter or record at the same time.

25–27 Underline the best answers:
Why was the typewriter so valuable in the office? (<u>records and letters became more readable</u>, <u>several copies could be produced at one go</u>, typists were cheaper to employ than clerks, it saved space, <u>it was quicker to type than to write</u>)

28–29 What do you suppose was the trouble with very early typewriters (before 1874)?

They were unreliable.... and ..expensive..

The teleprinter

[30–36]
Because of the growth in trade there was a need for a machine that would send printed messages quickly across the world. This machine would have to send a lot of information rapidly and accurately.

The telegraph, which used Morse Code and needed skilled operators, could not cope with the increased amount of information.

Although the telegraph went on being used for communication with ships at sea, a more efficient method was needed for major communications.

Following the invention of the modern typewriter came the **teleprinter**.

The typewriter had used an arrangement of levers to cause the type to strike the paper directly. The teleprinter used the keyboard to produce a coded series of electrical signals which could be sent along wires or by radio.

When these signals arrived at the receiving end, they were used to drive the appropriate type levers in a printer to print out the message.

Morse Code, which used different length signals to convey the message, was not very convenient for use with the new system, and a different way of coding the message was introduced.

30–33 What would you think would limit the accuracy of information sent by the

telegraph? ..The.signaller.had.to.convert.the.message.into.code..

and ..had.to.tap.out.the.code..

and ....the.other.signaller.had.to.receive.the.code.and.translate.it.back.into.letters

and ...write.down.the.message..

34–36 What would you think would limit the amount of information which could be sent

by Morse Code? ....The.speed.at.which.code.could.be.sent.

....and.received

and ....the.number.of.lines.along.which.code.could.be.sent.

and ....the.number.of.skilled.telegraphists.available

Teleprinter codes

[37–43]
The invention of the first teleprinter was probably by a Frenchman, Emile Baudot, who developed a method of sending five signals at the same time.

He originated a code based on fives, which coded the 26 letters of the alphabet, together with a space which was used to separate words.

He used two further coded signals which could shift the meaning of the codes from the letters of the alphabet to numbers and punctuation marks.

The signals from the keyboard could be sent directly and printed as they were received.

But they were usually used to drive a punch which perforated paper tape according to the code. This tape could then be read as it passed across five little levers which operated switches. Where there was a hole the lever dropped in, operating the switch – a **tape reader**.

The signals from the tape reader could be sent long distances and then used to drive a paper tape punch. The punched tape in turn operated a printer.

The tape reader and punch could operate faster than a person using the keyboard.

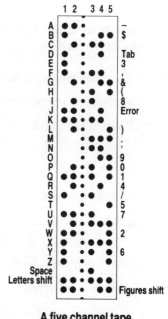

A five channel tape

Later, a way was found to send information in blocks of eight signals and the eight channel code was developed.

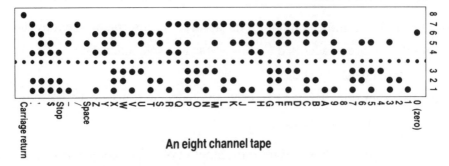

An eight channel tape

This method of coding and sending printed information has developed further and is still used today in the **telex** system. This provides a means of communicating the printed word over the telephone lines.

37–39 Compare the five channel code with the eight channel code. What advantages can you see in the eight channel code? ...More.control.characters.could.be.coded.. and ..so.could.punctuation.marks... and ...letters.and.numbers.could.be.coded.without. ...sending.an.extra.shift.character..

Underline your answer to question 40 from the words in brackets.

40 Using the keyboard to prepare paper tape *before* sending, and then sending the message from the paper tape, used the telephone or telegraph lines (<u>more</u> , less) efficiently than direct sending from the keyboard.

41–43 What other advantages can you see in preparing the message on paper tape and in receiving it on paper tape? ..It.can.be.checked.for.accuracy.. and ...then.sent.faster. ..(at.any.time).. and ....after.receiving.it.can.be.stored.until.read.or.until.it.needs to be referred to

Pictures by wire or by radio – facsimile machines

[44–57]
Fill in the missing words from this list:

sharp   picture   light   illuminate   information   microphone   signal
electrical   reflected   recreate   receiving   photoelectric   focused

In the telephone, the mechanical vibrations of the air, which are called sound waves, are converted to varying electric currents by a coil and magnet in a ....microphone.

The varying electric currents can be used to recreate sound waves by a coil and magnet in a headphone or loudspeaker.

Similar methods have been used to send a picture over long distances, either by wire, or by radio.

To convert a black-and-white .picture.. into ..electrical.. signals, it first has to be divided up into extremely small pieces. Each of these can then be measured for their blackness by a **photoelectric cell.**

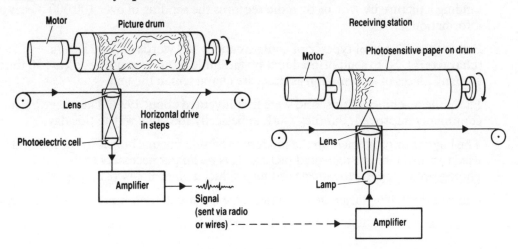

The photoelectric cell is a device which converts the light falling on it to an electric current, the .signal.. produced depending on the amount of .light..

The picture is usually wound round a drum, and is illuminated by a lamp. The light .reflected.. from a small portion of the picture is .focused.. onto the photoelectric cell.

Either the drum or the photoelectric cell is moved, so that the picture is scanned in lines. When one line has been examined, the drum is slightly moved and the process repeated so that the whole picture is covered.

The varying electric current produced by the ..photoelectric.. cell as it moves over the picture is sent, either along wires or by radio, to a .receiving.. station.

At the receiving end, a similar arrangement is used. Here, though, the photoelectric cell is replaced by a lamp which varies in brightness according to the varying electric current originally produced by the photoelectric cell.

Instead of the light which is used to .illuminate.. the picture in the sending machine, the receiving machine is kept in the dark, and instead of the picture there is a sheet of photographic paper.

The varying amount of light falling on the photographic paper as it is scanned by the light will .recreate.. the original picture when the photographic paper is developed.

To produce a ..sharp.. picture showing a lot of detail requires the individual pieces of picture scanned to be extremely small. So the scanning of the picture takes a relatively long time and a very large amount of ..information.. is required to be transmitted.

For example, a picture which is 10 cm × 20 cm contains no less than 20 000 squares 1 mm × 1 mm, or 80 000 squares 0.5 mm × 0.5 mm. The absolute minimum needed to produce a sharp copy of the picture is 80 000 × 0.5 -mm squares, so that sending a picture by wire or by radio requires the sending of over 100 000 pieces of information.

By contrast, a page of typescript contains about 400 words or 2000 letters (**characters**). So to send printed text by facsimile requires sending at least 50 times as many pieces of information as there are characters in the text.

Facsimile machines of this kind were first invented about 1920. They have been continually improved, but they work in basically the same way to this day.

The biggest improvement in the modern facsimile **fax** machine is in the method used to reproduce the recreated picture. It is no longer necessary to use photographic paper – the image can be produced on ordinary plain paper.

57 Can you think why facsimile machines were not much used for sending letters until recent years? ..Machines were expensive and slow..

Information storage

[58–65]
The offices in the first half of the twentieth century had many typists, who produced enormous quantities of paper and mountains of records. All of this needed storing and filing so that any information which was needed later could be found easily and quickly.

58 How are the names in the telephone directory arranged? ..In alphabetical order..

59–61 Can you suggest three ways that the information in an office could be arranged so that it could easily be found? ..In alphabetical order; by subject; in order of time.. ..or date received..

62 How does a table of contents help you to find things in a book? ..It directs you to the subject you need..

63 What can you use an index of a book for? ..To find particular items mentioned..

64 With a large amount of stored information to search through, would an index be essential? ..Yes..

As soon as we have a large accumulation of information we need a guide to lead us to what we want.

65 Indexes to large amounts of information, like the contents of a library or a set of filing cabinets, are often kept in the form of cards. Why is this so useful?

..Indexes are often added to. If they are on cards, new entries can be inserted in..

..the right place and old entries can be removed

The development of the digital computer

[1–8]
The first digital computer was a very elaborate calculator. It could perform extremely long and complicated mathematical and scientific calculations under the control of a set of instructions, or **program**.

The **input** was the means of putting the *raw* information into the computer, and the **output** provided a means of seeing and recording the results of the calculations.

The **arithmetic and logic unit** carried out the necessary operations on the information put into the computer – addition, subtraction, multiplication, division, comparison etc. It did this according to the instructions it received from the program, which was read and interpreted by the **control unit**.

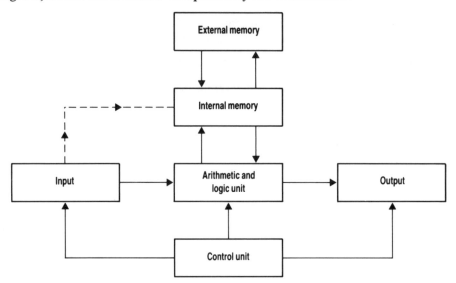

Any temporary storage could be made in the **internal memory** of the machine, and any results which needed to be referred to further were stored in the **external memory**. Computers of this type filled a whole room.

Modern computers have developed very rapidly since the invention of the **transistor**, which can be thought of as an extremely small switch.

It is easier to design electrical and electronic circuits as switches which only have two states, on and off. So the digital computer uses the binary system of counting – counting in twos – and the whole arithmetic and logic unit is arranged to use this number system. This is not unlike the Armada bonfires' yes/no in the last paper!

At the time, input and output to computers used the teletype. This had a keyboard to produce punched tape which could be read by a tape reader, and fed into the computer. Similarly, the computer produced its results on paper tape, and these could be subsequently printed on the teletype machine.

Teletype machines were using eight channel tape, and so blocks of information were read to the computer in groups of eight. With eight wires, eight lamps and eight switches, people could send any number up to 255 by operating particular switches. Like this:

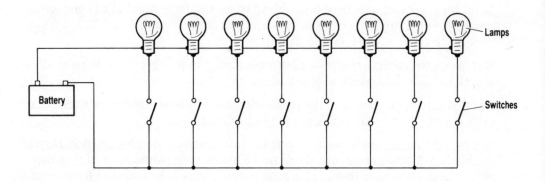

128	64	32	16	8	4	2	1	
0	0	0	0	0	0	0	0	(all the lamps off) will represent 0
0	0	0	0	0	0	0	1	(the first lamp on) will represent 1
0	0	0	0	0	0	1	0	(the second lamp on) = 2
0	0	0	0	0	0	1	1	= 3
0	0	0	0	0	1	0	0	= 4
0	0	0	0	1	0	0	0	= 8
0	0	0	1	0	0	0	0	= 16
0	0	1	0	0	0	0	0	= 32
0	1	0	0	0	0	0	0	= 64
1	0	0	0	0	0	0	0	= 128
1	1	1	1	1	1	1	1	= 225 i.e. 128+64+32+16+8+4+2+1

What will the following lamps switched on represent?

1 00000100 = ..4..

2 00001000 = ..8..

3 00001011 = ..11..

4 10000000 = ..128..

5 11111111 = ..255..

6 01000000 = ..64..

7 00100001 = ..33..

8 00010000 = ..16..

This provided an easy way to send numbers to the computer. Larger numbers than 255 could be dealt with by using more than one block of lamps and switches to describe or define the number.

Data processing

[9–14]

Computers soon became smaller, cheaper and more powerful. The increased power came because they worked faster and possessed a great deal more internal memory.

In recent years methods have been found to make a large number of connected transistors on a single slice of silicon – a silicon chip. So computers have become very much smaller, cheaper and more powerful.

But the digital computer had an enormous ability to process the written word (**text**) as well as to do mathematical calculation.

For this to happen, letters of the alphabet needed to be translated into the binary notation which the computer used for all its processing.

In 1966, the American Standard Code for Information Interchange (ASCII) was established. It works like this: there are 26 letters in the alphabet and they can be either capital letters or small. This requires 52 letters to be coded. There are also a number of other characters such as full stops, question marks and inverted commas, as well as the decimal numbers from 0–9, which need to be sent if a message is to be complete.

The total of all the characters which are needed in normal English communication is less than the 256 combinations which eight channels provide. So in the ASCII code, every letter, capital or small, every number 0–9, and every punctuation mark is given a number from 32 to 128. The numbers below 32 are reserved for special control information.

For example, 2 is start of text; 4 is end of transmission; 32 is space; 48 is the decimal number 0; 65 is capital letter A and 97 is small letter a. So if 00000100 = 4 appears it indicates that the transmission is finished.

To go back to our switches and lights, what combination of lights would you need to signal:

9 the start of the text? ....00000010....

10 a space? ....00100000....

11 the number 0? ....00110000 (32+16)....

12 a capital letter A? ....01000001 (64+1)....

13 a small letter a? ....01100001 (64+32+1)....

14 the end of the transmission? ....00000100....

[15–18]

Each piece of information – that is, the signal carried by one channel – is called a **bit**. The information carried by the eight channels is called a **byte**.

Information can be moved about the computer, transferred to a printer or sent to other parts of the system. When this is done on eight or more lines at once we call the information **parallel** – several bits are being transferred at the same time.

It is quite possible and often more convenient to sent the eight bits of information, which make up the complete byte, one after the other. This is known as **serial**.

This has two advantages: only two wires are needed to transmit the information rather than eight, and over long distances it avoids the danger that the signals sent on different wires might not arrive at exactly the same time.

The keyboard of a computer or electronic typewriter is really a collection of switches. When we press the space-bar, which is 32 in the ASCII code, the switch operated by the space-bar sends 00100000 to the computer. In the same way the switch operated by pressing 'A' switches the lines 01000001.

15 Why is it not reliable to send parallel information at high speed along very long wires? Signals sent on long wires may arrive at slightly different times

16 How many wires are needed to send *serial* information? Two

17 If messages have to be sent between two computers using telephone wires, the message will have to be sent in serial form.

18 If information is sent in serial form at a rate of 80 bits per second, how many bytes will be sent in a minute? 600

[19–26]
With simple switches quite a large number of operations can be controlled.

For example, let's look at this diagram:

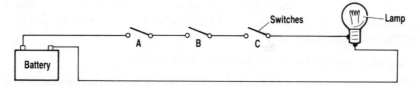

19 What do we have to do to make the lamp light? Close all three switches

20–21 If switch A is used to send the message, and switch B is open, will the information get through? No Will it get through if B is closed? Yes

22 If switch A is sending the message, how many other switches need to be closed to allow the signal to pass? Two

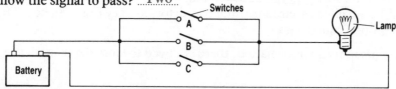

23 What will happen to the lamp if switch A is closed? It will light

24 Will the lamp light if any one out of A, B or C is closed? Yes

25 How many switches need to be closed to make the lamp light? One

We can easily arrange to turn switches on and off by an electric current.

Now, if switch A is operated to send the message:

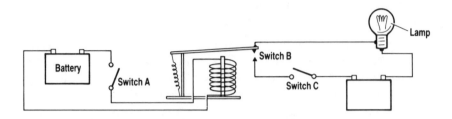

26   What has to be done to send the information to the lamp? .Close.switch.C...

Such arrangements of switches are much used in computers and are called **gates**.

[27–28]
The first combination is called an **AND gate**. It only allows messages to pass if *all* switches, which we call **inputs**, are closed – that is, if there are signals on each input. Signals will pass only if input switch A, input switch B *AND* C are closed.

The second combination is called an **OR gate**. It lets information pass from a signal on any of its input lines. It allows a signal from any one out of switch A, switch B *OR* switch C.

Transistors can act as switches in this way and can operate very fast. Combinations of these simple circuits control much of the organisation of information in computers and related devices.

Underline your answers from the answers in brackets.

27   An AND gate will pass on a signal when (all inputs, any input, no inputs) are switched on.

28   An OR gate will pass on a signal when (all inputs, any inputs, no inputs) are switched on.

Storage of information on the computer

As we have seen, information can be sent along wires in a simple code, and can be organised and controlled by circuits using transistors as very fast switches. This information is often called **data**.

At various points in using information, there is a need to store the data, to keep it for future use.

This storage is often needed only temporarily.

[29–34]
In the code which is normally used, a byte of information consists of eight separate bits, each of which are on/off or yes/no.

One way in which a byte can be stored is to have eight switches that are set to represent the data contained in the particular byte. This will remain until the switches are changed.

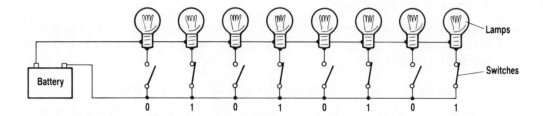

This is much the way in which a computer's memory works. Transistor switches can be arranged to stay set in a particular way until a positive move is made to change them. These are used in what is called **random access memory** or **RAM**. They all switch off when the power is turned off and lose the information which was stored. So when you switch on again, the RAM has disappeared.

Other transistor-based switches are designed to remain set in a particular pattern permanently. These are used in **read only memory** or **ROM**, and the information carried in ROM cannot be changed. They do not change even when the power is turned off.

Read only memory can be used to store the essential information to control the computer, the **operating system**.

The special set of instructions which translate what we might tell the computer to do into a set of commands which the computer can work with is called a **programming language**. This is often the BASIC language and it too is frequently stored permanently in ROM.

29 Why is ROM not suitable for data which the computer has to work with and change? The information in ROM cannot be changed by the computer

30 What part of the computer memory is best suited for data the computer has to work with and change? RAM

31 What does a programming language such as BASIC do? It translates our wishes into commands which the computer can work with

32 Why is BASIC often kept in ROM? It does not change and is always required

33 Why is RAM not suitable for permanent storage of information? It is lost when the computer is turned off

34 Why is the information stored in the computer's memory usually lost if the power fails? Because the transistor switches switch off when there is no power

Storage on punched tape or card

[35–38]
Transistor switch storage is not usually suitable for keeping large amounts of information for a long time.

Punched paper tape or punched cards were once widely used for this purpose. Each byte can be coded on paper tape by punching holes to represent the 1s and no hole where a 0 is coded.

This tape looks similar to the teleprinter tape illustrated on page 56.

Automatic punches were developed to punch the paper tape with the information sent by the computer. The data could be read back using light beams and photoelectric cells.

The reels of paper tape required to store large amounts of information were very bulky and punching the tape was comparatively slow. So paper tape and punched cards are now outdated.

35–36 Why was paper tape not very convenient? ...It was bulky.. and ..slow to punch or.. ..read..

37 Do you think punched cards were better or worse? .Worse..

38 Why? ....They..were.more.bulky.and.slower.to.handle.than.a.reel.of.tape.

Magnetic storage

[39–41]
The tape recorder uses the varying electric current produced by a microphone to vary the magnetic field on magnetic tape.

Magnetic tape consists of extremely small particles of magnetic materials glued onto a thin plastic tape. If you take a strip of adhesive tape, such as Sellotape, and sprinkle iron filings over it you can make a rather crude piece of magnetic tape.

Each of these particles acts as a tiny magnet. It becomes magnetised by the varying electric current passing through the recording head, which is a small electromagnet.

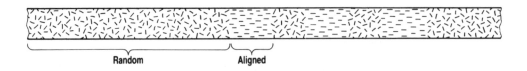

Random   Aligned

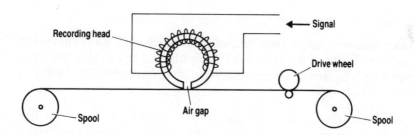

When the tape is played back, the varying magnetism of the tape causes a varying electric current as the tape passes the playback head (another small electromagnet). This current is converted back to the sound which you hear.

39 What produces the varying electric current in the first place? <u>The microphone</u>

40 Where is the varying signal stored? <u>On the magnetic tape</u>

41 Does the tape need to be played back at the same speed as when it was recorded?
<u>Yes</u>

[42–44]
This kind of information, where the electric current varies according to the pitch and intensity of the sound, is called **analogue** information. The variation in electric current is in proportion to the sound or other signal.

Computers usually provide **digital** information, with a series of coded yes/no or on/off signals. These are easily dealt with in magnetic recording, since all that is required is to magnetise or not magnetise the tape according to the information – magnetised = yes; not magnetised = no.

Nearly all the data that is generated by computers, and stored to be rearranged or used further, is recorded magnetically and in digital form.

Because the individual particles of magnetic material are so small, large amounts of data can be packed into relatively small amounts of magnetic material.

42 What does analogue recording mean? <u>The recorded signal is proportional to the</u>
<u>pitch and intensity of the original sound</u>

43 What does digital recording mean? <u>The information is recorded as a series of</u>
<u>yes/no signals</u>

44 Why can a lot of data be stored magnetically in a small space? <u>Because the</u>
<u>individual magnetic particles are very small</u>

Digital magnetic storage

[45–49]
For a long time tape was used for magnetically recording data. The difficulty with tape was in searching for specific items of information.

Have you ever spent a great deal of time searching for a particular track on a long cassette? You have the same problem with data tapes. To collect particular items from a long tape containing a mass of data means wheeling back and forth through this very long tape.

Modern data storage uses the magnetic material in the form of a disc. The data is recorded in a series of circles one inside another. The read and record head moves very quickly across the circles to collect information from all over the disc.

Because read and record heads and magnetic materials have improved, information can be packed more tightly on the disc. Now we have discs which can carry as many as 200 million bytes of information, which can all be easily and quickly accessed.

45 What is the main problem with using data stored on magnetic tape?

..Searching for what is wanted..

46 Is this problem as great, greater, less or just the same with paper tape?

..As great or greater..

47 Why is a magnetic disc more convenient than magnetic tape?

..It is quicker to move to a point on a series of circles than it is on a long, straight...

..tape..

48 What is the advantage of packing the information more tightly on a magnetic disc?

..More information can be searched with less physical movement of the read and..

..record head (i.e. it is quicker)..

49 Do you think that the data could be searched more rapidly on a magnetic disc than

on magnetic tape? ..Yes..

[50–53]
Underline the most useful answers:

50 A word processor is a (computer, computer with a special program to make it convenient to handle text, computer which can jumble words, modern typewriter).

51 A printer is a (printing press, machine which converts the signals it receives from a computer into the printed word, rubber stamp, paper tape punch, duplicator).

52 A disc drive is a (gramophone turntable, tape recorder, machine which records signals from a computer on a magnetic disc).

53 A keyboard is used to (<u>communicate with a computer</u> , store information, play
a musical instrument).

Communications

[54–60]
So far we have described the sending of signals by electric currents that travel along
wires. But wires have their problems as their length gets longer and the signals get
faster.

Modern computers work very fast, mainly because as they get physically smaller
the distances signals have to travel within the computer get shorter.

As we have seen, computers communicate by switching an electric current on and
off very rapidly. As this quickly changing signal passes along a wire, the on/off
edges of the signal become blurred until eventually, at the receiving end, the
message is no longer clear. The signals have run together.

The telephone lines that we have at present will rarely work reliably when the
information is passed at more than 1200 bits per second. This is very slow when
computers are capable of working and producing information at over 1000 times
that speed.

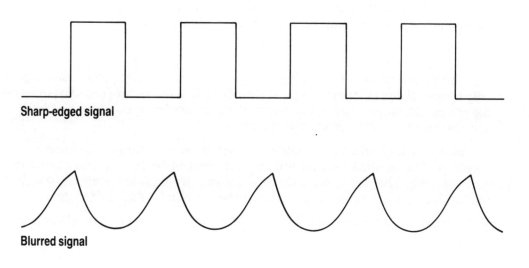

Sharp-edged signal

Blurred signal

54 What happens to fast signals over a long length of wire? .....They tend to run.....
.....together and get blurred.....

55 A high quality television picture may contain 1 200 000 bits of information. How
long would it take to send over the telephone lines? ....17... minutes ....approx. – 1000...
seconds.

Lasers emit light signals. Another means of communication uses this light. Light travels very fast and lasers can be switched very rapidly.

Strands of pure glass are drawn out into very long threads, fused together and given a special coating to keep the light within the fibres and to protect the glass fibres. These **fibre optics** will transmit light over considerable distances.

Light from a laser can be switched rapidly by a computer and shone in at one end of the fibre optic. The rapidly changing light level can be detected at the other end, converted back into an electric current, and used to pass the message to the second computer.

56 What other applications of fibre optics do you know? ..In various instruments..

..used to look inside the body..

57 Do you think direct communications between laser and a suitable receiver of light

would be possible over distances of several miles without using fibre optics? .Yes...

Underline your answers from the words in brackets.

58–60 What would limit communication of this kind? (amount of daylight, <u>rain</u>, <u>snow</u>, <u>fog</u>, none of these)

You might say, quite rightly, that television pictures contain a large amount of information which changes rapidly, so why not use radio or television communication to link computers and transfer information?

There are problems. One is that the amount of room in the airwaves is limited, as different signals have to be kept separate. Another is that high speeds of transferring information require high frequencies, and high frequency radio signals only travel reliably in straight lines, as light does. Therefore between two points on the ground the range is short, because of obstacles like trees, buildings and hills, and also because of the curvature of the earth.

The answer to high speed information transfer between computers is to use **satellites**. The satellites used for this are in an orbit where they remain stationary over the earth. They are also in a direct visual path from **ground stations**, which send and receive the signals and which may be thousands of kilometres apart.

Very high frequency signals can be sent to the satellite and relayed to other stations on the ground.

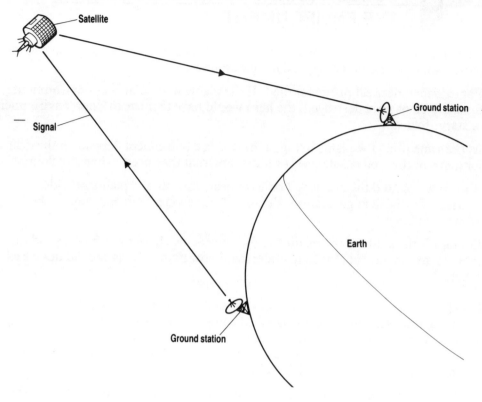

[61–66]
Underline what you think are the best answers:

61 The growing power of information technology depends (entirely, <u>a lot</u>, very little, not at all) on space exploration and the use of satellites.

62 The results produced by a computer are (always, <u>never</u>, sometimes, often) more reliable than its program.

63 Information technology depends (entirely, <u>a lot</u>, very little, not at all) on the computer.

64 The information produced by a computer is (always, never, sometimes, <u>often</u>) as good as the information it is given.

65 Computers are most useful for (playing games, storing large amounts of information, <u>rearranging and searching the information</u>).

66 It is (<u>useful</u>, essential, unimportant) to understand how a computer works and how to program it, before you use it.

PAPER 8 ECOLOGY AND PEOPLE'S EFFECT ON THE ENVIRONMENT

No living thing – plant or animal – lives alone. Animals and plants that live in the same area, or community, depend on one another.

For example, deer eat plants for food. If the plants in their area or **environment** disappeared or were destroyed, the herd would have to move to a new environment or starve to death.

At the same time, the plants living in the deer's environment depend on the deer for many of the food substances, or **nutrients**, that they need to live and flourish.

Animal wastes and the decaying bodies of dead animals and plants provide nutrients for the next generation of plants. Animals can limit and control the growth of plants.

Ecology is the study of the relationships living things have to each other and to their environment. It helps us to understand how living things depend upon each other.

[1–7]

All living things are made up of chemical compounds, which in turn are made up of atoms of carbon, nitrogen, hydrogen and often oxygen. To make new living material needs energy. The chemical changes that are essential to life take place when the compounds are in solution in water.

Water is a compound of hydrogen and oxygen atoms, so that we can say that the basic ingredients for life are carbon, nitrogen, water, and energy.

1   What is the primary source of energy for living things? The sun

2   Where is the most plentiful supply of nitrogen? In the air

Underline the answer to question 3 from the words in brackets.

3   The most immediate and useful supply of water for living things is (the oceans, rivers, lakes, <u>rainfall</u>).

4   Which living things can directly use solar energy? Green plants

5   Green plants can obtain the carbon that they need by taking in carbon dioxide

6–7   Animals obtain the carbon that they need by eating plants or other animals

The nitrogen cycle

Although nitrogen is so plentiful in the atmosphere, most living things are unable to absorb it directly and use it to make new cell material.

Before nitrogen can be used generally, it has to be in chemical combination with other elements.

As plants and animals die, their cell material breaks down or **decomposes**, freeing some combined nitrogen for new plants to absorb. This enables them to grow.

However, some of this combined nitrogen is converted to nitrogen gas, which escapes to the atmosphere and is lost as an available food.

Certain specialised bacteria, most of which spend their lives in close association with plants such as clover, live in lumps in the roots of these plants, called **nodules**. These bacteria *are* able to make chemical compounds from the nitrogen in the air.

The nitrogen from the air that these bacteria 'fix' is taken up by the clover and other plants and used to make new plant material.

This kind of close relationship, where different species live closely together for their common good, is called **symbiosis**.

[8–12]
Complete this diagram of the nitrogen cycle by adding arrows to show the direction of the flow of nitrogen.

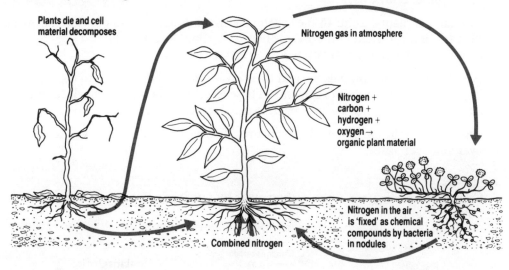

Rotation of crops

[13–15]
Farmers have always known that, if their land is continuously used for many years, the crop gradually becomes less and less as the nitrogen in the soil is used up.

To combat this they introduced a rotation of crops, through which they grew a different crop each year and about every fourth year planted clover. The clover was ploughed back into the soil, and as it rotted it provided new combined nitrogen.

13 Why would the combined nitrogen be much reduced if the same crop was grown for many years in the same field? _Much of the nitrogen would be taken up by the_

crops and not returned, as the crop would be removed from the soil

14 How else might the *modern* farmer deal with the problem of nitrogen shortage without rotating crops? ...By adding nitrogen compounds to the soil as fertiliser.

15 What other reason can you suggest for growing different crops in a field each year? (Think about plant pests and diseases.) ...To prevent pests and diseases, which ...often attack a particular crop, getting established

The carbon cycle

Another major need of living things is a supply of carbon. The element carbon, existing as soot, graphite, coal or diamond, cannot be used to make new cell material, but it can be used when combined with oxygen as the gas carbon dioxide. This gas occurs very widely.

Carbon dioxide is absorbed by green plants in daylight and with the aid of the sun's energy is converted by them into organic chemicals as new plant material. This is called **photosynthesis.**

Animals eat plants. Some of the carbon compounds are used to provide energy and the carbon is returned to the atmosphere as carbon dioxide. The rest goes to build new animal material or is excreted to return to the soil.

Finally, plants and animals die and their bodies rot and decay due to the action of bacteria and other micro-organisms. These use the carbon compounds for energy and the carbon dioxide escapes back to the atmosphere.

This is called the **carbon cycle**. It ensures that the carbon is conserved to be used over and over again.

[16–22]
Complete this diagram of the carbon cycle by putting in the arrows to indicate the flow of carbon compounds:

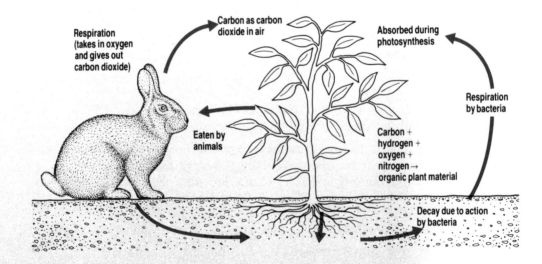

Food chains

The dependence of one small animal upon another is seen very clearly if we look at **food chains**.

In nature, animals usually eat only certain kinds of food. These animals are then eaten by larger animals which may, in turn, be eaten by larger animals still. This is known as a food chain and each living thing forming food for another is a link in that chain.

Let's look at an example in an undisturbed pond.

At the bottom of the food chain are the green plants, and they can be thought of as the **producers**. All the animals which feed on them are **consumers**.

As long as the pond remains undisturbed, a natural balance will develop, in which the numbers of the various links in the chain will be regulated by the amount of food available.

[23–27]

23 What will first limit the number of pike in the pond? ...The number of perch... ...available for food...

4–25 What two factors will prevent the number of sticklebacks increasing?
...The available water fleas as food... **and** ...the rate at which the sticklebacks are... ...eaten by the perch...

26 What do you think would happen if we caught a large number of sticklebacks? ...The water fleas would increase and the perch would starve...

27 What controls the total amount of animal life in the pond? ...The growth of the... ...green algae, which depend on the sun...

[28–33]
Real examples of food chains are likely to be very much more complicated than this. For example, the **food web** that we might expect to find in an uncultivated area of grass and woodland:

28–32 Even this is a very simplified version of what goes on in such an undisturbed area. Can you add five extra features to this food web?

33 What might happen to this food web if there were a long period of drought?

.The.vegetation.would.all.be.eaten,.and.then.the.beetles,.rats.and.rabbits.would..

.decline,.causing.the.foxes,.owls.and.stoats.to.hunt.further.afield...

The human race and the environment

[34–47]
Fill in the missing words from this list:

dioxide   fisheries   food   crops   climate   environment   disturbance
travel   greater   growth   balance   medical   manufactured   cultivate

As soon as humans ceased to become hunter gatherers and settled down to

cultivate.... the land and grow crops...., they started to affect the natural environment. For a long time the effect was fairly small but in recent times the

growth.... in human population and food.... production has greatly disturbed the

balance.... of nature.

The population of the world is much greater.... today than it has ever been. It is

increasing rapidly, partly due to vast improvements in medical.... science, but also because of improved methods of food production, so that fewer people die young.

But as the human population has increased so has the ..disturbance.. . The population had grown to 3300 million in 1968 and is expected to rise to 6000 million by the year 2000. These vast numbers need feeding and this means a growth in farming and ..fisheries..

Despite remarkable improvements in the efficiency of food production these numbers also require an increasingly large amount of land devoted to food production, especially in the areas where the ..climate.. is more favourable for rapid plant growth.

At the same time, people's increased expectations about their lives have led to a large increase in the amount of space they require to live, work and ..travel..

There are greater numbers of factories. The growing demand for ..manufactured.. goods means large amounts of energy are needed both to make them and to run them. The energy industries of today burn huge amounts of fossil fuels (coal and oil), releasing large amounts of carbon ..dioxide..

In modern times the effect of the human race on the natural ..environment.. has been overwhelming.

Effect of clearing the land

[48–50]
To make more land available for human food production and increased human living space, large areas of the world's forests have been cut down.

Other large areas of forest are being used to provide the vast amounts of paper and paper goods which we use.

Large areas of forest and woodland do more than provide a home for many species of animal.

They also efficiently convert large amounts of carbon dioxide into plant material. This is becoming increasingly important, because we are producing enormous amounts of carbon dioxide by burning oil and coal to provide energy. This adds to the 'greenhouse effect'.

Burning the forest produces huge amounts of carbon dioxide. Destroying the trees removes the 'factories' that would absorb the carbon dioxide and produce oxygen and animal foods.

The roots of the trees bind the soil and hold it together. The old leaves fall to the ground, where they decay and provide a store of useful nutrients.

48 How is the 'greenhouse effect' expected to affect the earth's climate?

  ..It is expected to make it warmer..

49 How will the destruction of large areas of forest make the effect worse?

.....Forests use a large amount of carbon dioxide as they grow

50 What may happen to the soil in an area where trees have been felled?

.....The soil may crumble to dust and be blown away by the wind or washed away by....

.....the rain.....

Dangers of intensive cultivation

[51–53]
If land is ploughed and planted and the crop is harvested when it has grown, most of the material which has gone in to the crop has been removed from the soil.

If the land is continually cropped, the essential nutrients for plant growth will soon be exhausted.

These nutrients can be replaced by adding fertilisers to the soil, but if they are simply applied as chemicals, then natural nutrients – mainly decaying roots and other plant material – soon disappear.

It is the natural organic matter in the soil which holds most of the water between periods of rainfall.

51 If land is intensively cultivated and only fertilised with chemicals, what do you think may happen if there is a long period without rain? ...The land may become...

.....dust and erode away...

52 How do you think that strong winds would affect the situation? ...They could make.

.....it worse by blowing away the soil.

53 How would you think that enclosing fields with hedges and providing clumps of trees might help? .The trees and hedges would form windbreaks to check the...

.....erosion of the soil by wind..

Air pollution

As the population grows so do waste products. When these waste products pile up they **pollute** (spoil) the countryside, rivers, seas and the air.

Fortunately, many countries are beginning to realise the dangers of pollution and are starting to try to deal with it.

[54–57]
The air is polluted with gases such as sulphur dioxide and carbon monoxide. Smoke – small particles of solid material, such as tar and carbon, in the air – is a considerable cause of pollution.

Much of this waste come from the burning of fuels in power stations and factories, as well as in car and lorry engines. The exhaust fumes of cars may also contain lead in a form which is harmful to life.

4–57   Underline the best answers from the answers in brackets:

Air pollution can be greatly reduced by (<u>conserving energy</u>, <u>making</u> <u>motor vehicles</u> <u>more efficient</u>, imposing <u>non-smoking bans</u>, using <u>more nuclear power</u>, using more electricity, using more coal).

Pollution of the countryside

[58–60]
Many plant and animal species in the countryside are being killed by pollution.

Pesticides and weedkillers have been increasingly used to control crop pests. The control of weeds and pests is necessary to produce sufficient food for our large populations.

Pesticides are usually applied directly to crops, where they are eaten by the pests, such as caterpillars, which feed on the crops. But these pests are also eaten by the next link in the food chain, so that the pesticides eventually find their way into larger animals.

Air pollution also *indirectly* pollutes the countryside.

Gases such as sulphur dioxide dissolve in the water vapour contained in rain clouds, and form acids. These acids are returned to earth, often many miles away, as **acid rain**.

Acid rain affects soil and forests growing on the soil. It drains into lakes, making them more acid and unable to support life.

58   What causes 'acid rain'? ....Gases such as sulphur dioxide, from power stations etc.,....
....dissolving in rain.

59   Why do farmers use pesticides and weedkillers? ....To kill pests and weeds and so....
....improve the yield of crops..

60   If scientists could develop less harmful ways of controlling pests, would this help to solve the problem? ...Yes..

Pollution of rivers and seas

[61–72]
Fill in the missing words from this list:

factories	washed	diluted	waste	poisonous	bacteria
harmful	lakes	climate	rivers	rain	dams

Need for water has led to the building of large ..dams.. and artificial ..lakes.. in some parts of the world. Some of these have been large enough to change the

environment and ..climate.. over quite a large area.

Rivers have traditionally been used as a means of getting rid of ..waste.. material. People have dumped waste into the river and allowed the river to carry the waste

out to sea where it is ..diluted.. in the vast volumes of the ocean.

Thus, ..harmful.. chemical wastes from ..factories.., sewage (human waste),

pesticides and weedkillers are ..washed.. off the land by the ..rain. and all find their

way into ..rivers. and finally into the sea.

Scientists are busy finding out ways of dealing with much of this waste, which has been dumped into rivers for many years.

For example, new kinds of ..bacteria.. are being found which can change

..poisonous.. chemicals into less dangerous forms. But dealing properly with difficult waste products costs a lot of money.

[73–75]
Waste materials are carried down to the sea by rivers, but one very serious cause of pollution at sea is oil. Most of the spillage of oil comes from accidents to ships which carry oil (tankers), and when serious damage occurs to a big, laden tanker a very large amount of oil can be spilled into the sea.

Oil does not mix with water but floats on its surface, so that a large volume of oil spreads to cover huge areas of sea.

The oil coats the feathers of sea birds and kills them as they try to get rid of it. It harms fish and as it washes up on the shore it covers the many animals that live at the shoreline.

Underline your answer from the words in brackets.

73 The size of the human population is the main cause of damage to the environment. (<u>True</u>, partly true, false)

74 Pollution is a product of human greed. (True, <u>partly true</u>, false)

75 Science can overcome pollution and damage to the environment. (True, <u>partly true</u>, false)

You will probably have noticed that you and your friends have many things in common and many differences as well.

If you have any friends who are twins (or triplets), or you are a twin or a triplet yourself, you will have observed something else as well. Some twins (and triplets) are identical and some are not.

We all begin life as an egg, smaller than the head of a pin. This egg, carried by our mother, is fertilised with sperm from our father. So we are a mixture of their qualities – how they look, speak, move and behave. Usually, one egg develops into a single person, but sometimes it becomes two or more.

Some **identical** twins are so identical that people have trouble telling them apart. This is because they developed from the same single egg in their mother's body, and have an identical set of **genes**.

The genes are the parts of the original fertilised egg which carry the plans of each human being, animal or plant.

When two *different* eggs are fertilised at one time, the children who are born are known as **fraternal** twins. They are not identical because they do not have identical sets of genes.

[1–6]
In your experience, state whether you think the following are true or false:

1   A brother and sister can be identical twins. .False...

2   People with blond hair always have blue eyes. ..False...

3   In a pair of identical twins, one can have blue eyes and the other brown eyes.

.False....

4   People with brown eyes always have dark hair. .False...

5   Freckles only come with red hair. .False....

6   Mary and Sara are sisters who look very alike. They have black hair and brown eyes. People often think Mary is Sara and vice versa. Mary's birthday is in March

and Sara's is in October. They cannot be twins. .True....

Each organism (plant or animal) which develops from a fertilised egg or seed has a set of characteristics controlled by its genes, which are special to itself.

Although each will be very like others of its kind, there will be differences. Dogs, for example, can range from tiny terriers to enormous St Bernards, yet all are dogs.

The reason for this individuality is that each organism receives half of its genes from its mother organism and half from its father.

So with every new baby or seedling, there is a special, new mix of genes, or plans. Each time genes are passed on, the mix from the parents is different.

While some of the children in a family may receive some similar groups of genes, like those for brown eyes or dark, curly hair, they may not look alike at all.

Although identical twins are special, it is just as interesting that everybody else is unique and so different from each other. People will resemble each other, of course, most closely if they are members of the same family.

[7–17]
Look at these pictures of different dogs, drawn to scale:

Which of these dogs would you choose:

7 as a guard dog? ..2..

8 to herd sheep? ..1..

9 to hunt small animals that live underground? ..4..

10 to hunt large animals ..3..

11 to race? ..5..

12 to protect flocks against wild animals? ..2..

13 Which of these dogs would you expect to survive a cold and harsh environment best? .1..

14 Which would you choose, for size and strength, to guard property? .2..

15 Which would you think originally came from a warm country? .5.

16 Does an animal that is meant to be a guard dog or a racing dog automatically become one? What else is needed? .Training.

17 Can you think of an example of behaviour that is automatic, even though training makes it more useful to people? .Pointers pointing; sheepdogs herding.

Each person has thousands of pairs of genes for many characteristics or **traits**.

Although a certain gene may not show up in that person, he or she may carry it and pass it on to a child, grandchild or even great-grandchild, when it suddenly may appear.

Two people with dark brown hair may suddenly have a red-haired child, and someone will say, 'Ah, yes, your greatgrandfather Smith had lovely red hair.'

[18–22]
Although they look very different from the outside, most animals are very similar in the organisation of their bodies.

Snakes, birds, reptiles, bears, apes and humans all have skeletons which are quite alike, as if they came from the same basic plan.

This could mean that many millions of years ago, there was a group of organisms from which they all developed, eventually becoming what are now quite separate groups of organisms.

18 Underline the correct answer in the brackets:

Suppose the skeletons of a snake and a lizard looked more like each other than those of a cat and a dog looked like each other. What would this suggest? (that the snake and lizard had a common ancestor, that the cat and lizard had a common ancestor, that the cat and dog had a near common ancestor, that the snake and lizard had a nearer common ancestor than the cat and dog had)

You will have noticed that, in your class, all the children have different coloured hair, eyes and skin. There will probably be a range of different heights, weights, strength, voices, body build and other traits.

19 If you are told that children get or **inherit** their characteristics from their parents, would you expect that you could get some idea of the way the parents of a class would look, by looking at their children? .Yes.

20 Why? .Because the children will inherit some of the characteristics of their. .parents and show a degree of likeness to them.

In a class of twenty 10-year-olds the following measurements are taken:

Eye colour:	Brown	Blue	Green	Hazel	Grey
Number with:	8	6	1	3	2

Hair type:	Very curly	Curly	Wavy	Straight
Number with:	3	2	5	10

Hair colour:	Dark brown	Black	Red	Light brown
Number with:	10	3	2	5

You will notice that there are lots of different hair and eye colours, even in such a small group.

21 Could at least one parent have had blond hair, even though none of the children has? ..Yes...

22 These variations exist in all groups of living things. There are only certain situations where the members of a species are exactly alike. In humans, this is when the people concerned are .identical twins... or some other form of multiple birth.

What happens in reproduction

[23–29]
The exact specification of a living organism is carried in the genes of the organism. A gene can be regarded as a plan describing some of the processes which are necessary to that organism.

The genes are arranged in long strings which are known as **chromosomes**, which we can say are like a book or scroll of plans.

A number of different chromosomes are collected together in the **nucleus** of each cell of the organism as a 'library' containing the complete specification of the whole organism.

Every time a living cell divides, new copies are made of all the genes. If all the copying has been perfect the new cells will each be an exact replica of the original.

However, in a small proportion of cases there will be a fault in the copy leading to changes in the offspring. Often the changes will be harmful to the offspring and it will not survive.

Occasionally the change introduced by a mistake in the copying will be helpful and the offspring will thrive, and give rise in turn to new organisms with the changed plans or genes.

These changes in specification due to faults in copying the genes are called **mutations**. They seem to be the way in which living things continually develop and improve.

When a whole plant or animal reproduces sexually, the **genetic material** of the female combines with similar material from the male. This forms new genetic material in the new organism, which contains a mixture of the characteristics of both parents.

Through reproduction which involves fertilisation of an egg by a sperm cell, or of an ovule by pollen in seed-producing plants, genes are being continually mixed up in different combinations.

23 Where is the 'library' of plans of any living organism carried? In the nucleus of the cell

24 Are these plans present in all the cells of the organism? Yes

25 How can they be changed as the organism grows? By mutation

26 Are all changes good for the organism? No

27 How is the genetic material continually mixed? By sexual reproduction

28 Does one gene carry all the necessary information about an organism? No

29 Does one chromosome carry a complete description of an organism? No

Natural selection and evolution

In the nineteenth century, scientists began to prove, through studying the earth and remains of much earlier times, that the earth was many millions of years old.

By their study of geology and **fossil** remains, they began to show that many layers of earth and stone contained remains of forms of life which had existed hundreds of thousands and even millions of years ago.

These fossils ranged from leaves retaining their shape in pieces of coal, through little sea horses preserved in amber, to the bones and skeletons of massive dinosaurs. The harder parts of animals and plants are best preserved.

Older layers of fossil remains showed simpler, often **extinct** forms of life. Extinct animals and plants lived once but can no longer be found on earth.

Sometimes a kind of life is found in fossils which exists in the same form today. If the organisms in this form have existed unchanged for millions of years, we nickname them 'living fossils'.

[30–36]
Underline your answer from the ones in brackets.

0–31 True fossils are (imprints of leaves and snails in pieces of coal, <u>small or large bits of organisms which lived long ago and are found in layers of rock or coal</u>, a kind of shellfish).

32 One of the most successful life forms which no longer exists today was the group called the (tigers, woolly elephants, <u>dinosaurs</u>, early ponies).
State whether the following are true or false:

33 Some fossil remains are similar to forms living today. True

34 Some fossils are totally unrelated to the forms of life on earth today. False

35 There are fossils of both animals and plants. ...True...

36 Fossil remains of shells are particularly common. ...True...

A scientist who contributed enormously to the understanding of living things was Charles Darwin, who took a famous sea voyage on the *Beagle*, which resulted in his book *On the Origin of Species* being published in 1859. This first stated the theory of evolution by natural selection.

From his studies of fossils and many observations on his travels, Darwin decided that living things are constantly changing. New descendants with slightly different traits are produced in each generation.

He also noticed that all life forms could produce many, many more offspring than could survive at any given time, given the supplies of food, water, natural enemies, and favourable or unfavourable surroundings. Only some would survive to become adults.

He said that at any given time the survivors would be those that were best equipped to deal with their environment, and that these would be most likely to produce offspring, which would be more like their parents, and less like those that did not survive so well.

Darwin called this process **natural selection** – the best equipped would be naturally selected to survive.

He also pointed out that the large groups to which living creatures belong are related to each other, and that all living things still have sufficient in common to have probably come from one single, simple ancestor.

[37–42]
Choose the most closely related pairs from this list:

domestic cat   elephant   tiger   spider   fly   horse   lizard   bat
mouse   bird   frog   grass   oak tree   lilac   wheat   fern

37 domestic cat and ..tiger....   **38** spider and ..fly...

39 lizard and ..frog....   **40** mouse and ..bat...

41 grass and ..wheat....   **42** oak tree and ..lilac...

In his **theory of evolution**, Darwin suggested that all life started as one form, and that gradually, generation by generation, it changed. Over millions of years, Darwin said, many very different forms have **evolved**, giving us the vast variety of life we know today.

The fossil evidence supports the theory of evolution, while the similarity of organisation in all animals that have backbones, for example, is strong **anatomical evidence** for the theory.

Further evidence comes from another source. People have studied how young creatures develop, from the earliest stages to being hatched, born, or whatever.

Human babies, for example, seem to go through the various stages of development from the simplest to the most complex life form. At one stage the human embryo has structures like the gills of fish. As the embryo develops, these disappear.

[43–51]
Underline the best answer in the following:

43 We now believe that life can only come from previous living creatures, seeds or eggs. (<u>True</u>, false)

44 According to Darwin's theory, plants and animals are related to one another. (<u>True</u>, false)

45 Darwin decided that a short, medium, <u>very long</u>) period of time was needed for one life form to evolve into the many different life forms in the world today.

46 Natural selection is sometimes called (everything comes to he who waits, <u>survival of the fittest</u>, a rolling stone gathers no moss).

47 Darwin's theory is also known as the theory of evolution. Evolution means (one government overthrowing another government; <u>gradual changes, development and progression of efficient life forms</u>; sudden changes in animal forms).

48 Frogs' eggs hatch into tadpoles. Do these have a different lifestyle from the adult frog? <u>Yes</u>, no

49 A frog is a (primate, fish, reptile, <u>amphibian</u>).

50 A tadpole in its early stages has many of the characteristics of a (water flea, <u>fish</u>, whale, sea horse).

51 Does this support the evidence for the theory of evolution? <u>Yes</u>, no

Plant breeding

[52–63]
Fill in the blanks from this list:

maturing   pollen   crop   flavour   qualities   appearance   luscious
fertilise   spreads   available   resistant   gardener

Among plants, breeders are often trying to 'add' good ..qualities... to particular kinds of plants.

By 'crossing' one kind of strawberry plant with another, using the ..pollen... from

one plant to .fertilise... an ovule from another, plant breeders try to combine two or more good qualities, and get them to occur in one plant.

We all enjoy strawberries in the summer. It used to be that strawberries were

mostly ..available... only in June. Now we have varieties which fruit much longer, or

have a second ..crop... in the autumn.

We have massive strawberries, strawberries with much better flavour, and strawberries which are more ...resistant. to the diseases which normally plague these plants. All this means that people can enjoy strawberries for a longer season.

Plant breeders who have the enormous food production industries in mind will often consider as most important the size, ..appearance.., yield per hectare, and reliability of the whole crop ..maturing.. at the same time.

Think of an enormous frozen-food company, which schedules its freezing factories to process peas one week, beans another week, carrots another week. A tasty, ..luscious.. crop of peas which matures in dribs and drabs throughout the summer just will not do! All of the peas must crop together for the greatest saving in running the freezing facilities.

The companies do claim to try to get the best ...flavour. as well, but if the best flavour belongs to an erratic cropper, then it may not be considered as a possibility.

Commercial dealers in seeds generally try to produce crops which are satisfactory to commercial food-producers, because of the tremendous size of the market.

The seed wanted by the home ...gardener.., however, unless he or she only wants to enter beautiful, even-sized vegetables in gardening competitions, is one that produces the best flavour and a good crop, which ...spreads. its ripening over a long period so that the family can make the best use of it.

Dangers of commercial breeding

A very serious question arises, both in seed production and in breeding of farm animals.

There is a tendency to breed from a smaller and smaller number of 'prime' plants or animals, and produce **clones**, or exact replicas of the originals, as much as possible.

This is meant to produce a much finer, stronger, better new generation of crops and/or farm animals. But it means that the variety of plant and animal types is limited.

The danger lies in reducing the **gene stock** to a very small selection, and possibly, unknowingly, gathering some 'bad' characteristics along with the desired ones. These would then be passed on to all the descendants.

'Bad' genes could mean anything from a shallow hip joint in an animal, too easily dislocated, to a very low resistance to a particular disease in plant or animal. Sudden contact with such a disease could wipe out large numbers of that particular population of plants or animals. Few would have different, resistant genes.

What we know about the particular genes, or combinations of genes, which control particular traits is still not enough for us to be overconfident about being able to 'breed' for better qualities.

In plants, where there may be a few restricted aims like larger cropping or greater resistance to certain diseases, we may succeed.

In cattle, where the breeders look for greatest production of lean meat and possibly faster maturation, to get them to market after the shortest time spent feeding them and looking after them, 'breeding' may succeed.

In pedigree dogs, overbreeding has sometimes led to unreliable temperament, so that dogs may bite without warning, or even to traits which are unhealthy for the animals (pug-faced dogs, for example, which may find it hard to breathe).

We find in fruit, vegetable and flower catalogues that the number of different varieties – even the number known to our grandparents – has reduced tremendously. Dozens of varieties of all sorts, from roses to gooseberries, have vanished.

At the same time many of the wild varieties have vanished or are in danger of doing so.

[64–69]

64   Why is there so much breeding of new crop plants?   To produce plants which are commercially successful

65   What can be done to preserve the gene stock of crop plants?   Keep stocks of a large variety of the 'wild' species

66   What can the overbreeding of dogs sometimes lead to?   Inherited physical defects; being highly strung

67   Why is there a tendency to breed from such a small starting group?   Trying to keep 'pure' breeds or 'best' characteristics

68   Why is it so important to have the wild varieties to go back to?   To keep up the gene stock's variety so as to keep from overbreeding and prevent inherited weaknesses or defects creeping in

69   Would a greater knowledge of the genes and the characteristics that they control make breeding programmes more reliable?   Yes